THE GOOD LANDLORD

**If you are associated with any of the following,
The Good Landlord will be of help to you.**

Condominium Associations
Cohousing Developments
Community Development Corporations
Employee-Assisted Housing
Expiring Use Properties
Group Homes
Homeowners
Homeowner Associations
Homeless Shelters
Housing Cooperatives
Housing Finance Agencies
Housing First Programs
Housing Investment Corporations
Landlord Associations
Landlords, Small or Large
Lodging, Boarding, and Rooming Houses
Multi-Family Housing

Nonprofit-Owned Housing
Online Real Estate Education
Property Management Companies
Public Housing Authorities
Rapid Re-Housing Programs
Real Estate Boards and Commissions
Real Estate Brokerage Firms
Real Estate Developers
Real Estate Training Institutes
Rental Housing Associations
Shelters for Adults or Families
Supportive Housing Programs
University Housing
University Real Estate Education and
    Certification
Veterans Housing

D1225539

Praise for *The Good Landlord*

Peter Shapiro's remarkable—indeed ground-breaking— book provides a treasure trove of good advice for landlords who want to make the world a better place. Combining both emotional intelligence and spiritual intelligence, The Good Landlord *uses narrative, sample dialogues, checklists, and even cartoons to teach how good intentions are not enough—skill in communication, relationship-building, boundary-setting, and negotiation are essential. Peter guides the reader—with specific, how-to examples—to a collaborative approach to being a landlord, one in which both relationships and results are pursued. Beginning his book with a quote from the Buddha and ending with eminently practical guidance on managing the eviction process while simultaneously pursuing a mutually agreeable settlement, Peter gives new meaning to the term "enlightened self-interest."* The Good Landlord *is more than just an essential book for landlords; it's a major contribution to the growing shelf of business literature that teaches people how to combine principles and profit, commerce and compassion—and how to do well by doing good.*

David A. Hoffman, Esq.
Mediator, Arbitrator, and Attorney at Boston Law Collaborative, LLC
and John H. Watson, Jr. Lecturer on Law at Harvard Law School
Boston and Cambridge, Massachusetts

Whether you became a landlord by accident or intention, you need this book to navigate the uncertain waters of renting. Our home, whether we own or rent, has a powerful emotional pull. Shapiro, with the wisdom of years of being a "good landlord," has written THE book on the subject of being a landlord (not a dirty word). Not everyone will or should own their home. Many need to rent. If you are currently, or are thinking about becoming, a landlord, please buy this book and read it, and by all means do the exercises. It will not only make you a better landlord, but a better person. Not many books can claim that! Shapiro's advice would have helped me avoid the problems I have had as a landlord. I only wish he had written it sooner!

Michael Jacoby Brown
Small Property Owner and Author,
Building Powerful Community Organizations:
A Personal Guide to Creating Groups
That Can Solve Problems and Change the World
Arlington, Massachusetts

This is an excellent publication that will be a great resource for any landlord, community development corporation, property management company, or nonprofit housing group. It offers an easy-to-read, well organized, and comprehensive overview of the key issues facing landlords, and will help them earn a fair profit while serving their tenants well and being a good neighbor.

Joe Kriesberg
CEO, Massachusetts Association of Community
Development Corporations
Boston, Massachusetts

Peter Shapiro's The Good Landlord *will help small property owners to manage their businesses more effectively, increasing profitability and lowering stress. Filled with thought-provoking ideas and time-tested strategies, this book offers landlords sensible ways to resolve tenant disputes while doing the right thing. Not an easy balance! With this highly practical guide, small property owners will find a way to address the most intractable tenancy issues they face. I highly recommend it!*

Esther Schlorholtz
Director of Community Investment
Boston Private Bank & Trust Co.
Boston, Massachusetts

The Good Landlord *is filled with good advice! Drawing on the most important ideas in the negotiation field, and tying them to real life challenges landlords face every day, Peter Shapiro clearly shows how landlords can meet their own interests while helping tenants to meet theirs. That's quite a feat, especially in hard times.*

> Larry Susskind
> Ford Professor of Urban and
> Environmental Planning
> at the Massachusetts Institute of Technology
> and Founder of the Consensus Building Institute
> Cambridge, Massachusetts

Learning new things and using that knowledge to solve problems are vital to the success of landlords, big or small. This publication provides perspective and insight on issues that owners can use to address problems on a daily basis.

> Greg Vasil
> Chief Executive Officer
> Greater Boston Real Estate Board
> Boston, Massachusetts

The Good Landlord *will help you keep the rent flowing without costly eviction disputes. Peter Shapiro's book shows how landlords and tenants can work together for their mutual benefit, and his extensive experience is evident in this excellent guide. Read this book: the valuable tips and techniques in* The Good Landlord *will ease your tenancy challenges—and save you money.*

> Chris Norris
> Executive Director
> Metropolitan Boston Housing Partnership
> Boston, Massachusetts

Landlords are stewards of the earth; we are just responsible for a bigger share of it than are others. For over twenty years Peter Shapiro has guided me to manage the challenges of leasing, handling repairs and negotiating with the many personalities involved with landlording. Peter has helped me maintain open communication and identify my long term best interests. The result? One hundred percent occupancy, full rent collections, no evictions, and positive relations with every tenant!

Now Peter's expertise is available to everyone in The Good Landlord.

> Paul E. Fallon
> Four-family Property Owner
> Cambridge, Massachusetts

I can't recommend Peter Shapiro's book The Good Landlord *enough! It is packed with invaluable advice and stories on how landlords can overcome difficult and challenging tenants in a positive way. Whether you are a new or a veteran landlord, this book will surely provide you with strategies to navigate the real estate business and put more profit in your pocket!*

> Tran Huynh-Mullaney
> Landlord
> Melrose, Massachusetts

In this timely work, Peter Shapiro offers property owners and the housing industry not merely a robust landlord guide but valuable insight into how to yield a return and thrive personally. The practical tips and strategies provide sound advice for improving the bottom line for landlords and tenants alike. Bravo for Peter's compelling argument as to how landlording can be a force for good.

> Alessandra Campo
> Landlord, Mediator and
> Tenant Stabilization Coach
> Malden, Massachusetts

My partner and I have had the privilege of being Peter's tenants in Jamaica Plain for the past seven years. Having witnessed firsthand Peter's application of the lessons presented in this book, we know they work! Peter is truly a fair-minded, responsive, kind and thoughtful landlord who also does well. If you are considering renting a unit out to tenants for the first time, or want to learn how to be a more fair-minded landlord and thrive, I recommend this book! Peter cares for his tenants as well as his own bottom line— and has many positive, long-term tenancies to show for it!

Melanie Hardy
Tenant
Jamaica Plain, Massachusetts

As one of Peter's tenants for the past five years, I can tell you that he is a good landlord! Peter allowed me to manage my tenancy in order to keep me financially secure throughout graduate school, a major surgery, and a stressful job search. I would not be in the stable position I am in right now, with a great job, without Peter's support. He is responsive to problems in the unit and willing to make improvements as needed. But Peter's not a pushover. He gets a return on his investment and has a healthy mortgage to pay! I'll never find a landlord I feel quite as comfortable with as I do with Peter!

Frances Harrell
Tenant
Jamaica Plain, Massachusetts

Peter is a down-to-earth landlord who practices what he preaches, and his principles are sound. I can vouch for this as his tenant and after reading his wonderful book, The Good Landlord: A Guide to Making a Profit While Making A Difference. *Peter is willing to listen, find common ground, and then make decisions that everyone is happy with, including him! This book is filled with useable information and advice that will help landlords to thrive by day and sleep at night!*

Alicia Eberle
Tenant
Roslindale, Massachusetts

THE GOOD LANDLORD

A Guide to Making a Profit While Making a Difference

Peter Gilman Shapiro

Part of the *The Good Landlord: Making a Profit While Making a Difference*™ Series

Published in the United States by The Good Landlord Publishing, Boston, MA.

Author: Peter Gilman Shapiro

The Good Landlord: Making a Profit While Making a Difference / *Peter Gilman Shapiro* — First Edition.

        283 pages
    Includes index

    ISBN 978-0-69-244036-0
    ISBN 0-69-244036-4
    Library of Congress Control Number 2015910125

Graphic Design copyright ©2016 by Nicky McCatty, signifyDesign

First Edition

Printed in the United States of America

*To my dad, Stanley Shapiro, who
first suggested that we invest together
in residential real estate, and who
has encouraged and taught me to be
a Good Landlord.*

Contents

Acknowledgments

This book has developed over many years working with and learning from colleagues, coworkers, experts, mentors, friends, landlords, and tenants, including my own! To them, I am grateful. The generous feedback, ideas and advice I've received have inspired me greatly.

I first want to thank my colleague and former coworker, Elizabeth Winston, who for over twenty years has tirelessly, competently and graciously devoted herself to the cause of mediating landlord-tenant disputes and preventing homelessness in Massachusetts. Elizabeth's joyful, upbeat attitude and her profound commitment to the cause have taught me an enormous amount. I am greatly indebted to her.

I also want to thank two mentors who have illuminated my work and encouraged me to write this book. Lawrence E. Susskind and Langley Keyes, distinguished professors at MIT's Department of Urban Studies and Planning (DUSP), have each challenged, educated and inspired me for over 25 years to expand my thinking in the fields of conflict resolution and landlord-tenant relations.

I also wish to thank another professor of mine, the late Donald Schön, for his wisdom and guidance throughout my graduate school days at DUSP. Additionally, two professors, Robert D. Putnam and (the late) Chris Argyris, whose courses I took at Harvard's Graduate School of Education, deserve praise. I also offer my sincere thanks to Frances Moore Lappé (author of *Rediscovering America's Values* and other writings), whose ideas have influenced me profoundly over the years.

I express my appreciation for Scott Brown, (the late) Roger Fisher, Sheila Heen, Deborah Kolb, Bruce Patton, Daniel Shapiro, Lawrence E. Susskind, and William Ury, and the other luminaries at Harvard Law School's Program on Negotiation (PON). I have learned immensely from these individuals, and from PON itself. The contributions these distinguished professionals have made to the field of conflict resolution are timeless and immeasurable. As many of the ideas contained in this book are credited to those at PON, I offer my heartfelt thanks and admiration.

I am grateful to Eliza Strode for providing invaluable guidance throughout this journey. Along with her partner, Dan Radin, Eliza stayed the course throughout as an editor, researcher, proofreader, technical assistant, and mentor.

I want to express my gratitude to a few individuals who read through earlier drafts of the book and provided ideas and editorial feedback. Thank you, Meg Alfoni, Michael Brown, Susan Craig, Bryan Tucker, Elizabeth Winston, and Gerry Zipser, each of whom helped me to get the words right. A special thanks also to Sam Case and Richard Cohen for their intellectual contributions. Thank you, Melissa Everett, as well, for helping me early on to draft some of the ideas contained in this book.

Thanks to my book designer, Nicky McCatty at signifyDesign, who devoted many hours to formatting and design. Thank you as well to George Michalec who, as the previous book designer, made substantial contributions to the interior and cover design. A special thanks to Jeremy Broekman, principal at Broekman Communications, for assisting with marketing, web design and communications.

I also wish to thank my colleagues at Metropolitan Boston Housing Partnership for collaborating with me over the years. Thank you Kevin Donaher, (the late) Mary Doyle, Steve Farrell, Kate Fulton, Aaron Korn, Sue Nohl, Chris Norris, Maura Pensak, Anne Rousseau, Jennifer Shaw, and the rest for providing the opportunity to partner in advancing the Commonwealth of Massachusetts' homelessness prevention goals.

Many other colleagues and coworkers have collaborated with and helped me to advance the ideas contained in this book. Thank you Ruth Bourquin, Elisa Bresnahan, Alison Bromley, Phil Bronder-Giroux, Kathy Brown, Doreen Bushashia, Gordie Calkins, Thomas Callahan, Ed Cameron, Brenda Clement, Sue Connelly, Chris Cotter, Lauren Curry, Sheila Dillon, Anna Dolmatch, Elizabeth Doyle, Annette Duke, Bruce Ehrlich, Kory Eng, Joe Finn, Evelyn Friedman, Stephen Fulton, Avi Glaser, Laura Glynn, Jim Goebelbecker, Laurie Goldman, Vielkis Gonzalez, Brad Gordon, Aaron Gornstein, Larry Gottlieb, Jim Greene, Soni Gupta, Libby Hayes, Rachel Heller, Roger Herzog, Henry Howell, Josh Jacks, Dick Jones, Chrystal Kornegay, Joe Kriesberg, Alan LaBella, Daniel LeBlanc, Tom Lorello, Robert MacArthur, Mac McCreight, Melissa McWhinney, Steve Meacham, Kelly Mulligan, Carl Nagy-Koechlin, Amy Nishman, Ashok Panikkar, Tom Plihcik, Doug Quattrochi, Jay Rose, Jerry Rubin, Skip and Lenore Schloming, Esther Schlorholtz, Diane Sullivan, Richard Thal, Kelly Turley, Joe Vallely, Greg Vasil, Kaye Wild, John Witt, and Clark Ziegler. And to the many others who have assisted me along the way, thank you as well!

Thanks to the leadership at Just-A-Start Corporation, the nonprofit community development corporation where I worked for over two decades. I would particularly like to thank Gordon Gottsche, Peter Graham, Peter

Munkenbeck, Deborah Ruhe, and Joe Youngworth for their support of my work.

Thank you to Luke and Theo, my two teenage sons, who have weathered my stories and quips about the world of landlording even when they didn't want to.

I give a special thanks to Aline Newton, my partner. Without her support and her patience, this book would not have been possible.

And most importantly, I wish to thank the many thousands of landlords, large and small, whose daily lives and contributions have inspired, touched and taught me for over twenty-five years. I have learned a great deal from each one of you who has strived in your work as a landlord to make a difference through providing decent, affordable housing. Your stories, lessons and insights have been crucial to this effort. Thank you!

A note about the names and stories in this book: In order to protect the parties' confidentiality, all names are fictitious, and all stories are composites.

THE AUTHOR GRATEFULLY ACKNOWLEDGES PERMISSION TO REPRINT THE FOLLOWING:

❐ *Mark Parisi Cartoons: Permission granted by Mark Parisi: ©Mark Parisi, www.offthemark.com*

❐ *"Ballad of the Landlord" from* The Collected Poems of Langston Hughes *by Langston Hughes, edited by Arnold Rampersad with David Roessel, Associate Editor, copyright ©1994 by the Estate of Langston Hughes. Used by permission of Alfred A. Knopf, an imprint of the Knopf Doubleday Publishing Group, a division of Random House LLC. All rights reserved.*

❐ *Leigh Robinson quote on pages 46–47: Permission granted by Leigh Robinson, author of* LANDLORDING: A Handymanual for Scrupulous Landlords and Landladies Who Do It Themselves: *11th edition (El Cerrito, CA: ExPRESS, 2014).*

❐ *Table, Share of rental units owned by individuals, 2001, on page 223, is adapted from Figure 19: Individual Investors Own a Large Share of Units in Small Rental Properties, and used with permission. Joint Center for Housing Studies of Harvard University,* America's Rental Housing—Meeting Challenges, Building on Opportunities *(Cambridge, MA: Joint Center for Housing Studies of Harvard University, 2011), 22. www.jchs.harvard.edu. All rights reserved.*

❐ *Much of the research in Appendix B: Alan Mallach,* Landlords at the Margins: Exploring the Dynamics of the One to Four Unit Rental Housing Industry *(Cambridge, MA: Joint Center for Housing Studies, Harvard University, 2007). Copyright by Alan Mallach. All rights reserved.*

The Good Landlord

The wise who are trained and disciplined
earn money
just as a bee gathers pollen
without harming the flowers.

They let it grow,
as an ant-hill slowly gains in heights.

With wealth wisely gained,
they use it for the benefit of all.

—Buddha

Introduction

What this book can do for you

If you're like most landlords, you stopped by one of your apartments earlier today to fix a stuffed toilet or clogged drain. You then called a tenant whose rent was late, and went to the bank. Perhaps you visited the hardware store to pick out paint colors— all in the name of serving your tenants, maintaining your building and making a profit.

And what about yesterday? That list included: attending a local playground fundraiser with your tenants, working out a payment plan, and clearing snow from a tenant's windshield so she could rush her toddler to a doctor's appointment. Whether routine maintenance or extra credit, these tasks *made a difference*—for your tenants and the neighborhoods where they live.

You may believe that *making a difference*—clearing snow off a tenant's windshield, extending payments for back rent by a few months, or supporting the local playground—will not help you as a landlord. Time is money. Furthermore, your kids don't use that playground anymore, you don't even live in the neighborhood and you choose your own charities!

This book will show, however, that *making a difference*—for your tenants and the neighborhoods where they live—*can actually increase your profits.* It makes good business sense for landlords to make a difference—*specifically, to meet the reasonable interests of their tenants.* It is through these intentional acts, glimpsed through the stories and lessons to follow, that you can achieve success! For example, when landlords are making a difference, they are:

- ❐ Helping most tenants, when they first become unstable, to avoid eviction if possible
- ❐ Making repairs, in many instances before tenants request them
- ❐ Considering the impact of their proposed rent increases on their tenants—and requesting reasonable increases when needed
- ❐ Negotiating access plans that respect tenants' privacy needs
- ❐ Accommodating tenants' needs to reduce costs per person by safely allowing additional occupants in exchange for higher rents
- ❐ Making it possible for tenants to have vibrant gardens on their properties without being a nuisance to the neighborhood

Whether landlords who do these things are "being good" or "making a difference," these examples represent responsible behavior for landlords seeking success. And when landlords succeed, they are making the **income** (see next page) they need while also enhancing benefits for their families, heirs, tenants, neighbors, friends, and the public at large.

When landlords are being good or making a difference, tenants often become more helpful, which can also enhance landlord success. For example, tenants will:

The Good Landlord

- ❐ Alert you that there's a water leak before major damage occurs
- ❐ Assist with minor improvements, or with errands related to fixing their unit
- ❐ Arrange contractor access either at odd hours or a moment's notice
- ❐ Be patient and flexible when repairs are needed and landlords can't respond immediately
- ❐ Police the premises and prevent crimes from happening

Tenants will be more likely to be helpful when their landlords are being good or making a difference. These forms of tenant cooperation will clearly increase profits for landlords.

In some cases however, the best thing landlords can do to meet their interests is to get the tenant out. Landlords can negotiate with tenants to move out on their own, using court enforcement procedures as backup. Landlords can also obtain an **eviction** order from the judge, and evict.

In other cases, the best thing landlords may do is not to grant tenants' specific requests such as to delay paying the back rent, add an additional occupant or leave their trash in the hallways. Landlords can use the practices presented in this book to determine how and when to set these boundaries.

DEFINITION: INCOME

Income is generally considered the money one brings in, such as rent. Income minus expenses equals profit. In the case of small landlords, profit reflects some mix of earnings for the time you put into managing your property and changes in the property's value, which may increase or decrease over time based on market factors, upkeep of the property, etc. I use the term *profit* in the title of this book to highlight that there are substantial gains to be realized when landlords are successful in their day-to-day management activities.

LEGAL INFO: EVICTION

Proper **eviction** procedures must be followed, and vary from state to state. See Appendix E. Landlords should research the laws in their state and follow them.

It is your decision, based on the conditions of your business, as to how much profit you need to make as a landlord. My purpose in this book is not to dictate how much profit you should make.

To help you make a profit, though, this book will discuss how to increase your success by expanding your definition of self-interest. When you meet the *reasonable interests* of your tenants and neighbors *as you meet your own,* your self-interests expand. You are meeting the interests of others to enhance your own bottom line. Throughout this book, I will call these your *enlightened self-interests.*

> **Refer to Enlightened self-interest, page 110**

It may not be immediately apparent that your success as a landlord is dependent on making a difference for others. By reading this book, however, this idea will become clear.

Is this kind of success possible? Absolutely. I have been pursuing my enlightened self-interests as a landlord for close to twenty-five years and have succeeded financially by carrying out the values of good landlording. Many other landlords have done the same.

When landlords act in their enlightened self-interests, they can:

▲ *Avoid difficult tenant battles*

▲ *Maximize tenant cooperation*

▲ *Make a profit while making a difference*

The next question, of course, is, "How?" How can a landlord make a profit while making a difference? How can you increase your profits by avoiding the need to evict a Section 8 tenant, for example, or by securing a workable access plan, or by getting your tenant to help you prevent water leaks? That's what this book is about, and I can summarize it for you here. It's about learning to deal well with people —their needs, frustrations and foibles. It's about motivating tenants to meet your interests as well as their own. It's about managing difficult situations without losing your cool. Mastering these practices can make a big difference.

These practices don't come so easily, however. There are many bumps in the road that can be quite costly in terms of time, money and stress. The good news is that these practices can be learned. The stories and lessons that follow offer timely advice to make the road easier and your profits higher.

You will also find examples of practices I call *super-good*. Super-good practices feature landlords helping their tenants, their buildings, the neighborhoods where their properties lie, and the public at large, *beyond what landlords need to meet their enlightened self-interests*. Whether landlords do this because their financial situations allow it, because they care and are generous at heart, or a combination of both, their contributions are valuable and worthy of respect.

Some super-good landlords, for example, have withdrawn many months of claims for rent to make it possible for tenants to avoid eviction. They have driven tenants to their medical appointments and babysat their kids. They have helped tenants access services and advocated for them. They have researched job leads and helped tenants write resumes. They have made substantial contributions to neighborhood improvement projects, and much more. As many of us contribute to the causes of our choice, these landlords have channeled their charitable resources and desire for social change into landlording itself. They have devoted their money, time and energy to improving the quality of life for their tenants, their neighborhoods and beyond. They are a force for social good.

Like the warnings that say "Don't try this at home," *you are not required to do what these super-good landlords do to be successful.* I cite examples of landlords who have lost lots of money and in some cases their buildings, due to pursuing super-good practices. You should consider these practices to be extra credit and to be done with self-awareness, although they are common to many landlords. How landlords invest their charitable resources is a choice they should make, not a set of concessions expected of them.

Why this book just on landlord-tenant relationships? Why a book on how to deal with people? There are many excellent books on how to invest in rental properties, choose the right management company and handle bookkeeping. However, in this business, it's not the maintenance or finance issues that can be most vexing. It's the people issues. The ability to deal with people is primary. And few if any books address in enough detail how to resolve issues with people, such as how to:

- Build effective landlord-tenant relationships
- Communicate effectively
- Negotiate based on pursuing interests over positions
- Address the issue of eviction using the principle of enlightened self-interest

Quite simply, if you can relate to tenants successfully, using the principles outlined in this book, you will be more likely to succeed as a landlord. If you can't, you are more likely to face large legal expenses, lost rent, and a lot of time worrying and having a bad experience. Ask Anthony, a landlord I worked with, for example. Anthony eventually sold his four three-family properties after facing one too many eviction disputes. Over the two decades I have worked with landlords, I've seen too many like Anthony lose their enthusiasm and zest for landlording due to these kinds of circumstances.

Two landlords

To make this real, let's look at two landlords, Mary and Helen, and the different approaches they use:

Mary

Wanting to be "helpful," Mary went out of her way to be generous to her new tenant, Caroline, a low-income individual with only a part-time job. By virtue of the new tenancy, and because of their close proximity in the same building, Caroline and Mary became friends. Mary kept the rent below market even though she could have used the additional monies to supplement her part-time teaching income. Because of her own limited resources, Mary fell behind on maintaining the unit. This didn't concern her, given the relationship she had cultivated with Caroline.

Despite the below-market rent, Caroline eventually fell behind in rent payments. Mary didn't pursue the back rent for a few months, given the financial pressures Caroline was facing. Reassured by Caroline that she would eventually "catch up," Mary let it go, trusting the rent would come soon enough.

Without any warning to Caroline, though, after the arrearage and Mary's financial worries had grown considerably, Mary one day abruptly reversed course. She asked Caroline to leave if she couldn't repay the back rent in a short time period. This angered Caroline, who assumed their friendship and Caroline's need to avoid becoming homeless was more important than money. Caroline stopped talking with Mary. This left Mary feeling betrayed and furious, and seeking revenge in a way she would have never expected.

Because Mary had extended a helping hand and been so generous, and was now owed over six months of rent, she felt it would only be fair that

Caroline move out. Mary asked. Caroline, however, had other ideas. Caroline decided to assert her legal rights. Mary would now need to go to court, requiring extra time and money she didn't have, to get Caroline out. She would have to hire a lawyer and face extended time in conflict.

All of this infuriated Mary unimaginably. To add fuel to the fire, Mary's eviction case was weakened by the fact that the unit had not been well-maintained. Caroline might be awarded enough **rent abatement** to have the case dismissed.

After many stressful and tedious hours being helped by a lawyer to prepare her case, Mary eventually did get Caroline out of the apartment. But Mary's costs were enormous: $4,500 in unpaid rent, $2,000 in lawyer expenses and court fees, some property damage needing repair, and her piece of mind.

Helen

Helen, by comparison, expresses little interest in being flexible if a tenant cannot pay the rent. She sees her role as a landlord as uncomplicated. Helen charges reasonable rents while keeping up with maintenance and repair and other landlord responsibilities.

When Natalie, a tenant of hers, recently fell behind on the rent, Helen called her after ten days and worked out a payment plan. To make compliance with a payment plan more likely, Helen made a deal with her. She honored some claims Natalie was making and withdrew a few hundred dollars of back rent. She also gave Natalie some needed storage space in the

---

DEFINITION: RENT ABATEMENT

A **rent abatement** or offset is essentially a valuation of the condition of rental property. In calculating a rent abatement, a court, at trial, can offset rent owed by evaluating the condition of the rental property. If the tenant can show the existence of code violations, the court can offset rent owed by ordering a rent abatement. If the conditions are extreme, the court can order the eviction case dismissed on the theory that the conditions more than offset any rental value of the property.

basement, which reduced a cost Natalie had been incurring to rent storage space elsewhere. But Helen initiated legal action as well, having failed previously to resolve eviction issues with Natalie without legal action. Once Helen worked out a payment plan with Natalie, she had their agreement entered into the court record as an enforceable order. *Helen was fully prepared to evict Natalie, and proceeded legally to do so if it became necessary.*

Helen and Mary—their differences

Helen's desire to be flexible smacks up against her belief that people should do everything in their power to be self-reliant, pay their own bills, and avoid handouts. Helen can afford to bend, however, and often chooses to do so. She doesn't consider it an obligation, but she gets satisfaction from helping. If Helen makes a deal the first time, and the tenant doesn't follow through, Helen will pursue the eviction in court *while keeping negotiations going*. Although Helen frets a bit over her decision to terminate the tenancy and proceed into court in short order, she does it easily enough knowing it serves primarily as leverage. Helen knows she can be flexible with her tenants when she has court as backup.

Helen maintains her units well, is consistent with her tenants, and treats them respectfully. She also makes concessions to give them a chance to avoid eviction. This flexibility not only benefits the tenants, but also fully protects Helen's interests, as she knows she can pursue eviction, and likely prevail, if necessary. Mary, on the other hand, emphasizes "doing good for those in need," but neglects maintenance while also being unrealistic regarding her own financial situation. In this case, she ended up in a dispute, furious with her tenant over lack of rent payments, though she had kept the rent very low. And Mary faced the risk of not being able to evict a chronically nonpaying tenant because she hadn't kept up with maintenance.

Purpose of this book

A primary goal of this book is to help you avoid misfortunes like Mary's. You will see the ways that relationships, like that between Mary and Caroline, can come apart—and how to prevent this from happening. A number of approaches introduced in this book can help you to deal more effectively with such difficult tenancies. Beyond using traditional legal tactics, landlords will discover a "secret ingredient of success," namely to build an effective working relationship based on trust, cooperation, and mutual respect. You will learn how to make peace with yourself while addressing difficult issues with your tenants, contractors, co-owners, family members, neighbors, co-workers, and everyone else!

The primary purpose of this book is to help landlords to make a profit while providing affordable, habitable housing. The approach I offer here can help you generate not only a profit, but a large dose of happiness, personal satisfaction, and renewed purpose as well! I present examples of successful landlords as well as lessons and practical advice to help you discover new ways to get positive results. I also include reflective questions at the end of each chapter for your own self-assessment.

Next, I'll describe my own journey toward becoming a successful landlord. My hope is that my own story and this book will help you avoid the many hazards of landlording and meet the goals you set for your own success.

The Good Landlord

With this book you can learn how to:

▲ Gain valuable skills needed to make tenancies successful

▲ Get better outcomes by communicating more effectively

▲ Strengthen your legal position as you deal with tenancy matters

▲ Maximize tenant cooperation when you need it most

▲ Handle eviction issues without spending extra time or money

▲ Develop your own path and forge your own identity as a landlord

▲ Maximize success with tenants, contractors, co-owners, and family members

▲ Gain more control, freedom, and peace of mind as a landlord

▲ Reach your highest potential for making a profit while making a difference

▲ Practice good landlording skills to make them real for you

▲ Achieve your goals and enjoy being a landlord!

A Guide to Making a Profit While Making a Difference

The Good Landlord

PART one

Making a profit while making a difference: The promise and the perils

1

My story

For over twenty-five years, I have been a landlord as well as a coach and mediator for landlords and tenants. My experiences have given me several unique lenses through which to view the landlord-tenant relationship. In this chapter, I want to discuss how I came to these professions and what I learned in the process.

Early in life, I began wondering how I could make a positive contribution to a world with such challenging and vexing problems. I opted out of the family paper box business started by my **great-grandfather** (see next page), in spite of the security it offered, and explored a wide range of vocations, including outdoor adventure education, fundraising, social work, community organizing, and sales. I traveled extensively in developing countries, worked with the less fortunate, and learned some ways to calm my mind—important skills for me at that time. Through it all, I was searching for a way to pay the bills, do some good, and express certain values that were uniquely mine.

Becoming a landlord

To my surprise, I have discovered that one of the most satisfying paths to these goals has been my work as a landlord. Like many other owners of real estate, I didn't plan to become a landlord. I had received a modest sum of money when my dad sold some business assets. Combined with my own savings at the time, I had enough to finance a graduate degree in urban studies and planning and to purchase my first "triple-decker" (three-family house) in Jamaica Plain, a neighborhood of Boston, Massachusetts. I made the purchase in 1990 (after viewing the building eight times, the last time at 3:30 a.m.). This was the same year I began working as a professional coach for landlords.

While I was first learning how leases worked and how to collect rents, I was also guiding my first landlords through their own conflicts in these areas. My early experiences as a landlord confirmed that it was possible,

A story: *my great-grandfather, Isaac Gilman*

My great-grandfather, Isaac Gilman, *who was born in Russia, arrived in the U.S. in the 1880s as a teenager. When he was 19, he started peddling papers and trinkets on the crowded streets of New York City. By 1907, he had enough money to take over a distressed New England paper company making newsprint and wrapping paper in the village of Fitzdale, Vermont. With Gilman's help, this northern Vermont hamlet grew from a handful of people to a modern community of 1,100. In gratitude, the town changed its name in 1913 from Fitzdale to Gilman. Isaac Gilman kept the mill running full-time during the depression, called his workers by their first names, took an interest in their personal affairs, and footed many a doctor and hospital bill. The Gilman Paper Company eventually moved to St Mary's, Georgia, and was recently sold.*

though not necessarily easy, to earn money while making a difference as a landlord. As a landlord and as a mediator, I have continued to explore how to succeed at this delicate balancing act.

Business with my dad

After hearing that I had bought my own three-family building in 1990, my dad suggested that we try some investing together. This came as a total surprise. Unlike my two older brothers who had worked in the family business, I had never worked with my dad before.

Upon reflection, I saw two possible benefits from this arrangement. First, working together could bring me much closer to dad in a way I had never explored. Second, my dad had a view of investing in real estate that was quite different from my own. Although I knew that investing in a three-family could provide long-term financial benefits, my original intentions were simply to secure ongoing affordable housing for myself. Dad, however, saw investing in real estate as a way to make money. Although I had never imagined or explored this approach, I felt I could benefit from his experience.

As luck would have it, on our first try we stumbled upon not just one, but two, triple-deckers. "Stumbled" is the right word here because completing the purchases took many unexpected twists and turns over many months. For example, we needed to buy both buildings at the same time because of requirements placed on us by the lending institution. And then a last-minute delay in purchasing one of the buildings led us to have to buy and sell the buildings to each other two extra times!

Although we believed that our mutual happiness would suddenly manifest once we were owners, we encountered a serious, unexpected conflict just days after we closed on these two buildings.

Still carefree at that time, I had been planning a long-awaited four-month leave of absence from my job, during which I would travel overseas. My dad, however, objected strenuously to these plans, insisting that I stay put in order to get our business off on the right foot. The buildings needed management and, because he lived in New Jersey and the buildings and I were in Boston, Dad couldn't perform this task. At the same time, I was adamant about adhering to my plans. We were at an impasse!

Finding a solution to this conflict required putting my mediation skills into practice right in my own backyard—between my dad and myself! I realized that he was correct in saying that our newly-acquired buildings needed good management. But I also realized that the management didn't have to come from me, at least not at first. As a compromise, I was able to convince my dad to hire, short-term, the person who was already the manager of one of the triple-deckers to manage both buildings. This would allow me to travel while giving us professional management while I was away. We were in business!

Over the years, owning property with my dad has been one of the most satisfying things in my life. The nature of this business requires that we be in continual contact. Semi-retired but quite active, my dad takes pleasure in being at his office. In fact, his personal adage is, "It's a good day when a man can put on his shoes and go to work." Dad keeps the books, makes the deposits, sends me useful ideas, explores new options, and offers advice on the details of investing. We talk throughout the week on financial and tenancy matters, making decisions as we go. Our real estate investments have brought us much closer while also contributing to our individual financial stability.

My first challenges as a landlord: Stories from the front line

As I emphasized in the introduction, of all the issues that landlords have to deal with, the most challenging are those involving people. Managing these challenges successfully, however, can bring significant rewards. Here are a few stories that illustrate how I learned to deal with difficult situations with various tenants.

1. *Turning things around through perseverance*

I have almost always enjoyed being responsive to my tenants' needs. This willingness to respond in a helpful manner has also produced positive business outcomes. One of my first attempts at this, though, challenged me greatly.

The tenant on the ground floor of the first triple-decker my dad and I bought was a low-income family of four, subsidized by a Section 8 voucher. This family with two young kids was clearly struggling day-to-day. There was a lot of conflict. The upstairs tenants regularly reported screaming incidents. At one point, the family was attacked by members of a gang who threw rocks at the building at 2 a.m. As my upstairs tenant reported by phone that night, confirmed later by police reports, they were hurling not just rocks but epithets, targeting my tenant's sister with whom some bad business apparently had been conducted.

In addition to these disturbances, paying the rent was sometimes difficult, given the family's financial circumstances. In spite of the challenges, however, I hung in there with them. I knew they loved the place and the neighborhood, and I believed they would eventually pay their rent. We enjoyed a good relationship—one which eventually led to a big improvement in the stability of their family.

I got an urgent call one evening from Juanita, the mom in this family. Juanita had been drinking too much. She confided that she was afraid that her husband might hurt her. She needed a detox facility immediately and was asking for help.

The way these detox facilities worked meant that you needed to advocate to secure a bed at the moment you called and you needed to get to it immediately. I made a rash of calls until I found one. I picked Juanita up and we arrived at the detox just in time for admission.

My timely action helped Juanita to regain her sobriety as well as her safety in the family. The unusual alliance we struck also helped restore her faith in humanity. Many people had abandoned her over the years. Juanita understood that I really cared. She called me regularly over the next few months, for support and also to request help to enter detox a few more times. Although I was asked to stretch quite far in this case, I knew how much it meant to her.

My actions also made sense from a landlord's point of view. I believed that my helpfulness would lead her to redouble her efforts to keep the place clean, get the trash out, pay the rent on time, and keep peace in the neighborhood—all of which did happen. Although in this case I did a fair amount of additional work to help my tenant, it made economic sense and gave me great personal satisfaction as well. I lessened the risk of property damage, which seemed likely, as well as possible eviction and turnover costs which could have been significant. My extra dose of helping, I figured, would protect my own finances, with the added benefit of increasing this family's stability.

2. *Keeping the peace within when responding to legal action, or: How to sleep at night when at war with your tenant by day*

I had not stepped foot in Tammy's unit since a brief visit to her apartment when I bought the building in 1998. The apartment featured a refrigerator dating back to the 1970s, creaky old windows, bulging walls, ancient carpets, and a very outdated bathroom. Given her low rent and her private nature, however, Tammy didn't want anything done, let alone seen, in her apartment. Period! She didn't waiver on this for years (although in hindsight I should have exercised my right to do periodic inspections, diagnose needed repairs, and make them). Over the years, I would see Tammy regularly at the local video store, exchange greetings, confirm that things were fine with her, and move on. And so it went.

Seven years later, however, I finally did hear from her—and loudly. The first missive came from the City of Boston Building Department. Concerned about air quality in her unit and potential effects on her asthma, Tammy had found her way to the building department. City officials promptly came out to do an inspection and I was soon served with six pages of habitability code violations spanning a wide range of issues.

My shocks were just beginning, however. The next day, I got a call from her lawyer informing me that Tammy would be withholding her rent. Tammy was asserting that I had known about these violations for the past seven years; therefore, she was requesting rent abatements going back for those years as well. Her lawyer was asking for $10,000 in compensation! I could pay this outright if she moved, or she could deduct it from the rent going forward.

My first reaction was profound disbelief at this sudden turn of events. My thoughts and emotions were racing. My feelings ranged from rage to betrayal to fear and anxiety, and, finally, to sadness. How dare she hire a lawyer and make such outrageous claims! Why didn't she call me first to resolve these concerns, knowing how accessible and responsive I could be? What if this cost me so much that I would have to sell the building? How can I handle this pressure given my myriad other responsibilities? I needed to pull myself together, and fast. Apart from the costs of the potential outcomes, the stress alone was debilitating.

Tammy's case turned on one document. Photocopied with a check I had cashed was a letter she had written when she first moved in that listed a few repair issues. She had actually written the letter not to initiate the repairs, but as part of a discrimination case she had filed against the previous owner. I had inherited this case and was able to resolve it quite easily upon taking ownership. But, in this instance, she claimed I had received this letter, which documented that I was aware of the repair issues. Of course, she had told me explicitly that she did not want the repairs, given her modest rent and her need for privacy, but I didn't have that in writing, and it wouldn't have mattered anyway. Instead, she was now seeking $10,000 because the repairs had never been done!

I knew this legal game all too well. As a mediator, I had watched hundreds of landlords go through similar experiences. I could start eviction procedures, face a battery of tenant legal defenses and spend many hours responding. I would need to hire a lawyer, which would cost a few thousand dollars. I knew I was vulnerable because of that letter, even if my tenant didn't write it to get repairs. And I was enraged because she had clearly been uninterested in any interventions during her entire tenancy with me.

Because landlords begin to feel outraged, betrayed, anxious, and much more from eviction cases like this, many choose to spend thousands of dollars in lawyers' fees to fight a case rather than to invest that money in the settlement process. *"I'll spend $5,000 on my lawyer before I spend a dime on that tenant!"* is the kind of rant I have heard many times from an angry landlord. But the consequences of taking this position can be many sleepless nights, court delays, and thousands of dollars in legal fees, all without any certainty over the outcome. Becoming overwhelmed by such strong emotions can lead landlords to make unwise financial decisions.

Knowing all this, I stepped back and spent some quiet time with myself. This was my first time as a landlord facing a rent-withholding case. I had a demanding, full-time job and was the father of two young children. If I negotiated my way out of this, I could probably manage my resentment, stay focused on my priorities, and spend just a little more than the cost of fighting it. I would also be able to sleep at night and live without months of rage and uncertainty as the legal process unfolded. I understood that Tammy's life wouldn't suddenly become easy with this windfall. I could pay her without feeling betrayed and manipulated by her for years to come.

I thus came to peace within myself. I settled for $4,500 and a plan to do the repairs. After living rent-free for a couple months, she would earn the rest through reduced rent payments. If she chose to move out, I would pay her any monies remaining. And I would be done.

Instead of spending many stressful hours fighting, and many nights tossing and turning over the hypocrisy of Tammy's choices and the audacity of her lawyer to ask for so much, I managed to treat this case dispassionately. It was a logical, strategic business decision. Maybe I could have saved some money and upheld a principle by fighting this battle, but in regard to my personal health, time management, and uncertainty for months to come, I would have lost the war. In this case, I chose the peaceful path—a choice I have never regretted.

This doesn't mean that landlords shouldn't fight sometimes. Indeed, I have waged my own fights and hired lawyers to help. The questions are when and how to do this. We will discuss these questions in chapters 10 and 11.

3. *Your lawyer can sometimes do what no one else can*

It finally became clear to me a few years back that Alan, a tenant of mine who had been living with roommates for over five years, was losing his edge. I had been invited more than once to mediate roommate disputes over noise, care of plants and kitchen duties. And needing to mediate disputes between my own tenants was something I did not want to have to do! I did it because it made good business sense at the time.

JIM AND I BOTH HAD A PET, AND SINCE THE LEASE ONLY ALLOWED FOR ONE...WE COMPROMISED...

Finally, after one too many blow-ups, the last one leading another clan of roommates to move out, I decided I had had enough. I asked Alan to leave.

Alan had other ideas, however. "I want to stay!" he shouted. And Alan made sure I heard him. Perhaps to prove he could succeed with roommates, he dug in. "This is my apartment! I've lived here for over five years! It is my right to remain here for as long as I want!"

I also became resolute. Because the rent had already been paid for the current month, I needed to file under "no-fault grounds" to be able to evict. The judge could award up to six months further tenancy before granting an eviction, but I could get Alan out eventually. If I wasn't paid rent the next month, I could add nonpayment as another claim in addition to **no-fault**.

As I took legal action, I also tried to talk with Alan. Despite my best efforts, I couldn't get anywhere. Alan remained adamant that he not have to move. His words became unpleasant. And he was interviewing roommates during this time! As trial day approached, I decided to get help. The day before, I hired a lawyer, briefed her, and paid her $300 to make an appearance. I was all set.

When we arrived at court on trial day, Alan was there. He had temporarily moved a few friends into the unit, I learned, which only enhanced my frustration. But this also meant I would be more likely to get paid next month's rent. I decided to offer Alan four more months, provided his rent stayed current, before I would evict him.

I approached him and began to speak. Alan, however, took center stage. He proceeded to rage for a few long minutes, flinging horrific insults regarding

DEFINITION: NO-FAULT EVICTION

A **no-fault eviction** means that a landlord is evicting a tenant for no stated reason. A landlord may not have a particular reason or he may have a reason but choose not to specify what it is. In Massachusetts, unless a lease specifies otherwise, the landlord does not have to state the reason, but must give the tenant 30 days' written notice of his intention to terminate the tenancy. Sometimes a landlord uses a no-fault eviction approach for strategic purposes, such as when he does not want to harm or worsen a relationship with a tenant or when he doesn't want to have to prove a "fault" ground at trial.

my personal character and landlording behavior. I stood there, barely breathing, witnessing an attack of embarrassing proportions. It eventually ended without any exchange of offers.

I turned to my attorney. She motioned to Alan, and both repaired to an adjacent room, presumably to negotiate. They emerged a few minutes later. Alan walked away. I asked what happened. "He wanted four weeks," my attorney told me. "That's all he wanted. He'll pay his rent, and leave. You'll have your unit by March 1st. I'll write it up, you both can sign it, and the judge can approve it as an **enforceable agreement**.

I was shocked to say the least. From wanting to stay forever, Alan did a virtual about-face and agreed to move in short order. The only explanations I could muster were my willingness to endure three minutes of being yelled at, and the fact that an attorney did my bidding. Alan had had his day in court, namely to hurl insults at me. He had also been able to "save face" by not having to face his perceived enemy to make the concession.

So, let this be a lesson. Your willingness to be a little humiliated and to use a stand-in can make all the difference. Not just when you need to advance your legal rights, but when you need another person to face your tenant, your lawyer can do things that no one else can.

4. Don't expect gratitude

One of my first tenants, Eric, lived in his unit for over eight years during which time I never raised his rent. I chose not to raise the rent because he was easy to work with, I knew him personally, I didn't spend much on any

---

DEFINITION: *ENFORCEABLE AGREEMENT*

Enforceable agreement in this context means that both parties have a written statement of the terms of their agreement, both understand the terms, both voluntarily have agreed to the terms (meaning no one unfairly pressured the other to agree), a court (usually a judge or clerk of the court) has determined that the terms do not appear to be illegal or unfair, and both parties willingly signed the agreement. Once a court approves this agreement, it becomes an enforceable order of that court and both parties must abide by it. If either fails to do so, the one harmed by the other's behavior can seek enforcement in the same court and ask the court to order the other party to comply or to impose penalties for not complying (depending on what the agreement spells out).

improvements, and I was new at the business. By the time he moved out, I had honestly forgotten if I was holding a payment for the last month's rent. (Since then, I have carefully documented receiving all payments of the last month's rent.) Eric claimed I had received it; I claimed I hadn't. And although he paid me in money orders, I didn't have any receipts. Neither of us had proof.

In the end, he decided not to pay his last month's rent. I protested at first, but then had another idea: I would forgo pursuing his last month's rent (although in my heart I believed I had not received the payment), in exchange for an acknowledgment from Eric that he had had a good deal for eight years. I wanted to be appreciated as a good landlord.

To my dismay, Eric refused. "You think I enjoyed living in this unit all these years with its low ceilings, floors scratches and the like?" he said gruffly. "I also remember quite well the two weeks when that construction debris sat in the side yard. You should be happy I paid the rent given those conditions!"

I was shocked! My experience confirmed that the unit was quite adequate and didn't warrant the criticisms. In regard to overall condition and rental costs, the unit compared favorably with hundreds I had seen. I had also been good to Eric, letting him into the building on occasion when he misplaced his keys, and responding immediately on the repair issues he requested. And I never raised the rent! Nevertheless, he didn't want me to think that I was helping him the least bit, even if it eased our way into a deal that favored him financially.

I learned an important lesson from this experience. You may think you're being helpful as a landlord, but your tenant assumes you're making a healthy profit off his rent. He assumes that your property value is rising rapidly, there isn't much work to do, and all you need to do is to kick back while the rent rolls in—and you leverage the building to buy more property!

Although there is another reality—foreclosures of rental property in Massachusetts alone were at an all time high of 9,000 in 2009—tenants tend to hold on to certain views about your role as a landlord. They believe that being a tenant puts them at a significant disadvantage.

Whatever the truth is, you can grow old trying to convince a tenant that you've been helpful—even if it's obvious! From the point of view of the tenant, this is their home. Each detail about their home life matters—especially how vulnerable they feel when faced with eviction.

When you make concessions to tenants, most tenants think these concessions are fair because they feel their position is inherently much weaker than yours. According to them, you hold the power and stand to profit. The least you can do is to charge below-market rents, allow an unauthorized occupant to move in, take out their trash, repair their property damage—and let them break their lease in the middle of the winter! To them, that's all fair.

So, the lesson is: don't expect gratitude from your tenants. If you help them, do it without expectation. This attitude will then allow you the occasional pleasant surprise when a tenant does appreciate your help.

5. *Coming to peace when your tenant doesn't call back*

Tom was a good carpenter, which made me confident I could barter work for rent if necessary. Tom had just completed a few carpentry jobs for me, he was friendly, and he needed a place to live.

Soon after he moved in, however, it became apparent that when the rent was due, Tom often wouldn't pay it—nor would he communicate with me. If I called to ask about the rent, he wouldn't call back until I called a few times.

It was hard to have to pressure Tom all the time, but I had no choice if I wanted to get paid. The situation was infuriating, but the biggest challenge was to keep my voice calm. Tom's personality simply couldn't handle anger. Raising my voice was not an option if I wanted to collect the rent. Getting compensated depending on keeping the peace.

Learning to maintain your equanimity in the face of resistance from tenants may be the most important skill you'll ever learn as a landlord. It's also one of the most difficult. You may not have imagined needing psychology skills to be a landlord, but the truth is, those are exactly the skills you need. In this case, each time I finally was able to make contact with Tom, I knew I would succeed if I kept the peace within. This wasn't easy given my profound frustration over his lackluster response. I needed to breathe through my anger and listen when instead what I really wanted was to shout at him.

Refer to Losing your cool, page 66

Discovering the greater value provided by landlords

As my career as a landlord began to expand, I also became a volunteer mediator at a local courthouse. Soon I began to mediate between landlords and tenants on the issue of eviction. What I saw deeply challenged my assumptions about the balance of power in these situations. Although one would think landlords could prevail easily enough if owed enough back rent, tenants' use of legal rights could reduce a great deal of this back rent, and stop evictions altogether. I saw landlords who had accommodated tenants in need—extending time to pay the back rent, tolerating nuisances, and allowing sublessees as a matter of course—but who still fared miserably in court.

Because they had stretched, I found out, these landlords were left legally and financially vulnerable when their tenants turned to the legal system and accessed attorneys. Being "nice" cost these landlords dearly, often to the tune of thousands of dollars in unpaid rent, legal fees, and property damage. In addition, they had lost faith that they could make a difference and make a profit, which for many had been their routine business practice.

My concerns grew for the predicaments of those landlords for whom an adversarial landlord-tenant relationship could cost them a great deal of time, money and stress. I began to wonder how these landlords could address their tenancy issues earlier as a way of improving their bottom lines. I also began to see how many small property owners, whether or not they saw their businesses this way, were providing front-line protection against homelessness. Besides keeping their units affordable and being flexible when the rent was late, many took a further step, offering help in very personal ways. This included driving tenants to job interviews, advocating for them, and helping them get social services. In short, they were doing "social work." Each time, they swore they would never do it again, but they kept doing it over and over, in spite of themselves.

Here's how one landlord put it: "This wasn't what I had in mind, and sometimes I think I'm crazy for doing it, but I don't see any way around it if I'm going to keep my business healthy. And I know that my tenants appreciate it greatly when I help them out. So I get something too!" I've heard similar messages from many hundreds of other small landlords with whom I've worked.

Over the years, I have gotten to know an enormous variety of people who happen to be landlords. I have been struck by the sincerity and conscientiousness of many. At the same time, I have noticed a naïve quality in some landlords as they manage tenants day-to-day. This book was conceived from my desire to make things easier and more profitable for these "mom and pop" businesspeople. It was also conceived from my yearning to encourage the good instincts of these landlords to be "helpful" whenever it makes good business sense.

This book arose out of a desire to offer sound, time-tested advice on how landlords can deal more effectively with challenging people problems. My advice is designed not only to make it easier for landlords, but to help them thrive in a world where many landlords, particularly the small ones, are at risk.

Becoming a professional mediator

To improve my capacity to help small landlords, I pursued graduate studies at M.I.T.'s Department of Urban Studies and Planning. My masters thesis explored effective approaches, whether using lawyers or not, to helping both landlords and tenants when eviction loomed. Both parties face risks when the tenancy becomes unstable. By the time I was finished, I was convinced that helping landlords and tenants to manage conflict could be one of the most powerful strategies for maintaining stability in rental housing. Since then, my work in counseling landlords has only strengthened that belief.

As a counselor and mediator, I have welcomed the opportunity to bring together people with opposing values and views—and, often, dramatically different degrees of political and economic power. I now run a mediation and legal services program at a nonprofit community development corporation, Just-A-Start, in Cambridge, Massachusetts. We are dedicated to helping landlords and tenants resolve their disputes, and to stabilizing housing for both landlords and tenants at risk of economic loss and homelessness. More often than not, my colleagues and I are able to help disputing parties discover solutions that improve their relationships. This happens not because we are human relations wizards, but because we have studied methods that work, have practiced them with discipline, and have gotten results.

Mediation has offered me a tool to help landlords get what they want and need, in a way that also satisfies tenants. It has allowed me to serve effectively with respect to both landlords' and tenants' situations, balancing the power in a way that can improve outcomes for both.

The specialized small property owner services we provide, as well, have provided me with a fulfilling way to make a difference for this important part of our housing sector. I know now that this is what I was searching for in my younger years. In this profession I am at home.

Looking ahead

In this chapter, I've presented a few different stories about how I learned to deal with difficult situations as a landlord. In future chapters, I'll discuss in greater detail how to handle these kinds of challenges and, even more importantly, how to avoid them in the first place.

First, however, let's look at a few more stories about successful landlords. In the next chapter, you'll see three such stories: two about small landlords and one about a large landlord. These stories demonstrate clearly that it is indeed possible to make a profit while being fair and helpful to your tenants. You can do both—and achieve great satisfaction in the process.

Questions for reflection: Your story

1. What led you to become a landlord?

   _____

   _____

   _____

2. Consider your own history as a landlord. At present, are you where you wanted to be when you started out? What might you want to change right now?

   _____

   _____

   _____

3. What are your goals as a landlord? These goals could be anything from dealing with tenants more easily to acquiring more property.

   _____

   _____

   _____

4. How would you prioritize your goals?

   _____

   _____

   _____

5. Recall a few disputes that you have had with tenants. Jot down a few notes about how you handled them. How well did you do?

   _____

   _____

   _____

6. When you have tried to be helpful to your tenants, have you felt stretched between your business interests and your concern for their difficult situations? Have you been burned when you attempted to be helpful? Jot down some notes on this.

   _____

   _____

   _____

2

Case studies:
Three good landlords

No enterprise can exist for itself alone. It ministers to some great need, it performs some great service, not for itself, but for others; or failing therein, it ceases to be profitable and ceases to exist.

—*President Calvin Coolidge*

In this chapter I will introduce three different landlords who are making a profit while making a difference. Two are small landlords and one is a large landlord. I put the large one, Jim, in the good landlord category, as he is making a profit by pursuing his enlightened self-interests. One of the small landlords, Jerry, however, used super-good practices over the years until he got burned one too many times, at which point he withdrew from these practices. The other small landlord, Mike, has used super-good practices throughout, while consistently making a profit.

As each of these landlords makes a profit, each is meeting his enlightened self-interests in unique and successful ways. Jim, for example, is proactive in approaching maintenance and repair. By proactive I don't mean just that repairs are handled promptly. Jim makes improvements in tenant health and safety, energy conservation, and other such matters *without being required to do so.*

All three landlords also help stabilize their tenants when their tenants are at risk, before eviction becomes inevitable. Each understands how valuable it is not only to help these tenants to avoid eviction, but also to save money, time, and stress. Each landlord, in his own way, makes the effort. Let's meet these landlords.

A former insurance salesperson seeking ways to become more entrepreneurial, our first landlord, Jim, started buying up properties in the late 1960s. He now owns over 500 units throughout the metropolitan Boston area. I met Jim at a courthouse where I provide mediation for eviction cases.

A Navy veteran and a super-good landlord, Mike, bought his first property on the street on which he lived when he was in high school. I met Mike at a landlord support group I run in Boston. A firefighter by trade, Mike owns five four-unit buildings (20 units), on the South Shore of Massachusetts. Mike also owns a rubbish removal business.

Jerry, co-owner with his brother of an auto parts recycling business, did a lot of super-good landlord practices until he got burned. I met Jerry when he approached me to go through his first eviction process after 40 years of ownership. Jerry bought his first "three family" building, just north of Boston, from his grandparents in the late 1960s. He bought it to live in with his young family. After buying another two-family, he eventually moved out of the three-family but has kept both buildings for long-term income.

What these landlords do

To whom do these landlords rent?

Jim's tenant population includes a large student base combined with a stable group of seniors, and many professionals as well. Jim understands the demand for student housing and recruits students successfully.

Mike's tenants are primarily disabled veterans, many of whom have rental subsidies. "I can relate to these guys," Mike tells me. "I was in active combat in Viet Nam for seven years and know what they've been though. I know what it's like for them now. I want these guys to be housed responsibly, which is the service I provide."

Jerry has rented, more often, to low and moderate income families. His buildings are situated in poorer neighborhoods. Aware that these families too often get "stepped on," Jerry has prided himself on being a source of housing for them. "I have done whatever I can," he told me, "to keep my rents reasonable." Not having much of a mortgage makes a big difference in his ability to do this.

A recent decision to rent to a particular tenant provides an example of a super-good practice of Jerry's. After a city inspector warned Jerry not to rent to a particular tenant, Jerry did anyway. "I've been helping these tenants for years," Jerry told me. "This family was no exception. People have 'read me' quite carefully, however," he then confided. "They know I'm an easy touch." The tenancy his inspector warned him against unfortunately backfired. Going through eviction led Jerry to change his approach.

How does each think about profit?

Originally Jim thought he would profit most by a process known as **flipping properties**. A mentor of his, a fellow landlord, urged him to hold on to his real estate "like a dog holds on to its bone." "I wasn't getting real traction," Jim told me. To this day, Jim holds on to his properties as a long-term investment. Jim makes a healthy profit from his properties, enhanced by his attention to his enlightened self-interests.

DEFINITION: **FLIPPING PROPERTIES**

Flipping is a term used to describe purchasing an income-producing property and quickly reselling (or "flipping") it for profit. The term also can be used to describe fraudulent or unethical practices used to meet short-term profit goals.

The Good Landlord

Mike knows that, by converting to condos, he could increase his profits. Mike is motivated, instead, to hold on to his properties and pass them on to his kids when the time comes. In the meantime, holding on to his properties allows him to provide an important service for the community, something which he values highly. Mike makes enough to pay his bills and then some, but he stops there. "I earn a basic amount above my expenses to keep me going," Mike told me.

Jerry also makes enough to pay his bills and then some. "Jewish practices advise you to do **mitzvot**, or good deeds," Jerry tells me. "The people I've rented to live close to the bone. If, in my small way, I can help out, I'm happy to do so." Jerry's mortgage is low enough that he doesn't need to max out on the rent, and he knows his tenants are stretching to pay what he charges. As a result Jerry keeps his rents moderate and doesn't raise his rents very often.

How does each approach maintenance and repair?

Fearing that a fire could wipe out a sizable population of young people in a 100-unit building Jim owned, he installed, proactively, a sprinkler system, although he was not legally required to do so. "I wanted to be able to sleep at night," Jim told me. Jim has been proactive in other buildings as well, improving safety systems, installing fire protections, hanging fire code sheetrock and more, all beyond what is required by code. Although one may call this super-good, to Jim such investments come naturally. "I know it benefits the tenants," Jim reminds me, "and ultimately it will pay off for me."

DEFINITION: MITZVAH

Mitzvah (plural mitzvot) is a moral deed performed as a religious duty. The word has also come to express an act of human kindness or generosity.

Jim also considers his tenants' needs when responding to certain maintenance situations. For example, if a tenant has to wait more than two days for a drain to be cleared, Jim will give her a fifty dollar credit. "These tenants care deeply about how they get treated, particularly regarding the quality of their housing," Jim told me. "Although they like the money, what the money tells them, they remind me, is that I care." Jim then says with conviction, "And I know that this understanding, that I care, reaps untold dividends! It takes a big bite out of that belief that landlords will hurt tenants in the name of profit!" As we'll learn later in the book, this type of deposit into what I call **the tenant relationship bank** can pay huge dividends to landlords down the line.

Refer to Making deposits into the tenant relationship bank, page 145

"I used to get twenty maintenance calls a day in 1975," Mike told me. His proactive maintenance plan has changed this, however. Mike can now go six to eight months with barely a phone call, which could qualify as super-good business practice. Even after maintenance is handled, though, Mike continues to help his tenants, and where it really matters. "I'm in the rubbish business," he reminded me. "I can get all my tenant's furniture for free, and many of them need it. I clean out residences and bring my tenants furniture that's like new, better than the thrift shop. I have three dump trucks, which I can use after hours." This clearly qualifies as super-good.

Steeped in the business of maintenance as an auto parts recycler, Jerry also cares about doing timely maintenance. His "can do" attitude is definitely an asset. "If I can fix things immediately, it makes me happier," Jerry confided. "I know what it means to the tenant."

How do these landlords handle the issue of raising the rent?

Jim is quite careful. He raises his rents regularly, but only two or three percent at a time. Furthermore, he may go two, three or four years without raising rents. "I want my tenants to stay," Jim tells me. "Turnover is very expensive." As a result, some tenants have been with Jim fifteen to twenty years.

Mike also sees tenancies as a long-term proposition. "I want their tenancies to be long-term, I've told them. And that's what I've fostered. Many tenants of mine have stayed with me ten, fifteen, twenty years." Mike didn't mince words when he told me, proudly: "I've treated them the way I want to be treated." Mike raises his rents only moderately. The rent paid by his tenants with **Section 8 vouchers** is a certain percentage of their income. The remaining percentage is paid by the agencies that administer the vouchers. Thus, rent increases do not overburden the tenant but are shared equitably between the tenant and the agency.

Jerry generally keeps rents at reasonable levels. Many books encourage rent increases, but Jerry hasn't followed this advice. He did acknowledge his expenses and how they go up on a yearly basis. Jerry, however, assumes he

---

DEFINITION: SECTION 8 VOUCHERS

Section 8 refers to a federally sponsored rental subsidy program for low-income tenants. It refers to both project-based and tenant-based subsidies. In the project-based subsidies, a tenant's rent is subsidized, but the subsidy stays attached to the unit and the tenant cannot use it if she relocates. In the tenant-based subsidies, a "mobile voucher" is provided and the tenant finds his/her own privately-owned apartment. The tenant pays about 30% of household income toward the fair market rent and the rest is subsidized, usually through a public housing authority, private landlord or nonprofit housing agency. The Section 8 program has limits on what it will subsidize, based on local prevailing fair market rents, size of the tenant's household, specific apartment conditions, and other factors. For example, since fair market rents are lower in Flint, Michigan than in New Haven, Connecticut, the upper limit subsidy for a Section 8 tenant in New Haven will be higher. Also, if that tenant is a family of two, they are free to rent the four-bedroom apartment, but their subsidy will cover only the fair market rental value of a one- or two-bedroom unit.

will avoid costly turnover and gain needed tenant cooperation as a result of not raising his rents every year.

How do these landlords deal with the issue of eviction?

Jim knows, when dealing with eviction, that his first move is to try to avoid it whenever possible. He regularly refers tenants to agencies that provide social services, housing services, and income supports. Jim will also include a letter inviting the tenant to try to work it out. "We nurse them along," Jim told me. In response to one woman Jim had rented to since 1983 who fell behind on her rent, Jim recounted: "It's her home. I try to respect that." Over the forty-plus years that Jim has been a landlord, it has been very rare that he has needed to evict anyone, although he will do it if and when he needs to. Jim will collect "eighty cents on the dollar," forgo a month or two of rent, or do whatever else is needed, within reason, to avoid eviction.

Mike also sends tenants a letter if they fall behind on their rent. He knows the Section 8 program staff will send a letter as well, which gives him leverage. "I've had a few bad ones," Mike told me. "I've brought them to court. The judge asked them to move." Mike, however, has lost very little money over the years due to nonpaying tenants.

Jerry had not needed to go to court for 40 years, until recently when he sought my help. Although Jerry's tenants have almost always paid up, things have changed, he told me. "I've rented to a new crop of 'professional tenants' who know how to avoid responsibility and avoid paying rent. Whether because they can't afford things, how they were raised as kids, or just because they can, some tenants just know what to do to avoid paying the rent. I just can't trust some of them anymore because of these experiences. I've been tainted! I have learned, in recent years, to be more careful. Things have changed."

What gives these landlords satisfaction?

Jim makes the extra effort to help his tenants, which is satisfying. "I'll get a tenant who could have been hooked on drugs and alcohol, but after we work together to stabilize his housing, his problems magically seem to straighten out," Jim told me. Jim knows he is making a difference, which clearly sustains him.

Mike rents almost exclusively to tenants with Section 8 vouchers, which is satisfying and, surprisingly to many, quite lucrative. Because the money is guaranteed, Mike trusts things will work out with the veterans to whom he rents, even if troubles arise. Mike, as a firefighter and a Navy veteran, reaches out to these veterans because he knows what they've gone through. "I lost a brother in 1974 to a fire in Quincy," Mike told me. "It was a very cold night. My brother's lungs collapsed." Mike knows these veterans care, which motivates him to be helpful. "They appreciate life a lot more than the average person, which is why I like to rent to them." Mike told me. Mike also feels proud to drive by his buildings and see that they are well maintained. "It's a good feeling of accomplishment," Mike tells me. "I get positive comments from the neighbors."

Jerry's emphasis on mitzvot, the doing of good deeds for others, drove him for years to accommodate tenants in need. Jerry has now changed his ways, having faced one too many difficult situations. Although Jerry always understood the income potential his buildings could offer, he told me, "I had other interests having to do with mitzvot. Perhaps I wasn't landlording effectively enough in the past," he confided. Although he was meeting his "humanitarian" interests, his stress, loss of personal peace, and his dwindling pocketbook caused a change in his behavior. He is more careful about his cash flow now, and pursues his enlightened self-interests more.

Can you pursue your enlightened self-interests and thrive?

Each landlord, in his own way, makes central the pursuit of enlightened self-interests, a concept that will be explored throughout this book, especially in Chapter 7.

Whereas for Jim monthly profit is more central, this is less important to Mike because of the long-term profitability of his buildings. Although profit was not central to Jerry's business approach, it is now, given his recent experiences.

Each, in his own way, thinks about repairs before the crisis hits. Each also considers the impact of a rent increase on his tenants, and makes most rent increases modest. And each tries to work with tenants, as a first step, before needing to evict.

What is common to all is their understanding that, in most cases, meeting the reasonable needs of their tenants makes it possible to meet their own needs. Whether they can be flexible due to their modest mortgages or because it makes good business sense, they all know the importance of making tenancies work. These landlords are by no means exceptions to the norm of landlording. There are many landlords who, like Jim, Mike and Jerry, consider the reasonable needs of their tenants. They have "done the math," and know that the investment of meeting their tenants' needs will undoubtedly pay off.

The Good Landlord

Although each assumes a long-term view of their properties, they also understand the value of month-to-month success. Although the fact that their properties are "good investments" is an important reason why these landlords can be super-good, there is certainly more to it, as we have learned. These landlords are each, in their own unique ways, making a profit while making a difference.

3 Landlording in the 21ˢᵀ century

Of all the people in the world, who's more detested than the landlord? After all, he raises rent whenever he pleases, he ignores tenant complaints, he keeps at least one cockroach colony in every rental dwelling, he loves the fresh air which broken windows provide, he welcomes rodents of all kinds to make their nests in his rental properties, he takes no pity on tenants who suffer misfortunes, he drives unfortunates from their homes, he sneers when others laugh, he laughs when others sneer, he dallies with divorcees, he drives an ostentatious Cadillac car, he runs over stray dogs and cats and blames them for not running fast enough to get out of his way, he wears a big black cape, and he smokes smelly cigars.

And if that landlord happens to be a landlady — well, then, everybody knows what she's like! She's got a schnoz longer than Pinocchio's, larger than a wicked witch's, and she puts it into every tenant's business. Her ears rival Dumbo's, and they're ever on the alert to learn the latest gossip. She's privy to Big Brother's personal findings on everyone, and she blabs them everywhere. She's devised ways to pinch her pennies that Scrooge never dreamed of, and while there may not be snakes growing in her hair, big pink rollers sure do.

—*Leigh Robinson*, Landlording

One spring day, at a local fair in my hometown, I came across a booth called "Dunk the Landlord." Hung over a wooden cask filled with water was a sign for "Scrooge Landlord." Onlookers were invited to strap into the seat harness below. Another person hit the side flapper, suddenly dunking this "landlord" into cold water. Written on the flapper were statements such as: *"Too much rent!" "Fix your building!"* and *"No more evictions!"*

Dunk the landlord! Take your shot; humiliate him; make him pay for the inhuman acts only a landlord could do. Take your rightful place, landlords, next to society's criminals, sleazy politicians and corporate crooks—anyone who has terrorized the innocent. This is the plight of the stereotyped landlord.

Landlord stereotypes

Highlighting the negative side of landlord behavior has been a habit in the media since perhaps World War II. Consider these headlines:

> *Slumlord strikes again! Refuses to fix boiler despite citations*
>
> *High and dry! Landlord shuts off water after tenant complains*
>
> *Landlord's thugs throw tenant in the street!*

But why do we rarely see headlines like these?

> *Delinquent tenant drives landlord into foreclosure despite large nonpayment and property damage; lengthy court procedure to blame!*

> *Tenant threatens landlord with knife to avoid rent payments!*

> *Tenant's boyfriend leaves neighbors reeling after late night party! Thousands in property damage reported!*

There certainly are landlords who do bad things, as there are tenants who do bad things. Given the profound influence the media can have on public perceptions, highlighting negative landlord behaviors in the press can easily produce landlord stereotypes. Unfortunately, simply by being a landlord, you have been stamped with a poor public image! Let me describe my own experience with being stereotyped.

"Whom have you been evicting lately?"

Early in 2001 I needed to sell a triple-decker I owned to generate income to pay expenses for my family. Because major renovations were necessary, I needed my tenants to move out sooner than planned. Knowing that they, like many, would expect to receive **consideration** in exchange for moving out quickly, I prepared to offer money, the amount depending upon their move-out date. My plan was to secure timely move-out agreements, informed by the law, which would meet both their interests and mine, and be satisfactory to all.

DEFINITION: **CONSIDERATION**

Consideration is anything of value promised to another when making a contract. It can take the form of money, physical objects, services, promised actions, abstinence from a future action, and much more. ("Consideration," *Wikipedia*, accessed April 12, 2015, https://en.wikipedia.org/wiki/Consideration.)

The Good Landlord

Here's what I worked out: One tenant began moving out on her own after a month. Another stayed for four months paying half the rent. The third tenant stayed for four months paying half the rent and then relocated to another unit I owned for a six-month stay paying full rent. I knew I could have ultimately evicted this third tenant in a shorter time period. Instead, I chose to make my concessions up front, while making sure that this tenant—and the other two—understood their **rights** and felt comfortable with the agreements reached.

A month later, I ran into a neighbor who had learned about the tenants moving out. "Hey, look, Harry Bennet's here," she joked, referring to a local slumlord known for his unscrupulous practices. "Who have you been evicting lately?" It turned out that she had circulated a neighborhood petition condemning my actions and demanding that I stop evicting tenants! She had also been talking up my "unethical" practices to some local community leaders I knew, while pressing her neighbors to take action.

I was quite upset to say the least. I felt angry, humiliated and treated disrespectfully. Everything I stood for as a good landlord—being flexible, improving the neighborhood, giving my time to worthy causes and, in this case, making sure each tenant felt satisfied with the move-out plan—all this felt invisible and invalidated, let alone misunderstood.

LEGAL INFO: *RIGHTS*

Massachusetts General Laws (M.G.L.) c. 239, sec. 9 (Stay of Proceedings) provides that in a no-fault eviction, a judge may grant a stay of proceedings of up to six months; if the unit is occupied by a handicapped person or someone age 60 or older, the stay may be granted for up to 12 months. However, the court must deem it "just and reasonable" to grant the stay, and the tenant must not be in violation of the lease nor owe rent. What is just and reasonable is determined on a case-by-case basis. For example, if a parent with a handicapped child wanted to keep the child in his current school and needed more time to find an apartment in the school district, that would tend to be "just and reasonable"—but maybe not if the landlord could show that the parent had not made any effort to search for a new apartment and many were available for a similar price in the district.

Every day, landlords and tenants reach agreements that tenants feel are fair, and which respect the law. And every day, as landlords earn their income, many also make concessions that provide support to tenants at risk of homelessness. Although I believed I had made a difference—for my tenants, the neighborhood and the public interest—I was publicly judged as having caused harm to others. And I was found guilty without a trial!

Refer to A typology of landlords, page 212

More stereotypes

In this case, I was the victim of a stereotype. The woman circulating the petition simply assumed I had evicted my tenants without having even bothered to talk to them, let alone having made sure they understood their rights. What do these negative public images show? For starters, they show how much the public misunderstands the vital role landlords play. They also demonstrate the need to educate the public better about what landlords do. They should serve to remind you not to be driven by public misperceptions. By maintaining effective relationships and approaching

Here are some other stereotypes that get placed on landlords:

▲ Landlords don't need to work hard. They profit without needing to invest much time or effort.
▲ Landlords earn money based on other people's (i.e. tenants') work and efforts rather than on their own.
▲ When tenants and landlords work together to improve a neighborhood, reduce crime, and strengthen neighborhood associations, the resulting benefits accrue only to the landlord.
▲ Landlords can neglect maintenance, discriminate, gain access without tenant permission, and order tenants out, all without due process or legal consequences.

The Good Landlord

disputes skillfully, you can continue to make a profit and make a difference for your tenants and the communities you serve. In so doing, you will not only be helping yourself, but you will be doing your small part to change the conventional image of landlords.

Strangely enough, being negatively stereotyped also represents an opportunity: if you are a good, let alone a super-good landlord, you'll stand out and probably be appreciated *all the more* by your tenants, who will usually show their appreciation by being good tenants in return. Although it may not be surprising to you that effective landlording requires hard work and a generous spirit, it might well be surprising to your tenants and the public at large.

Of course, the image of most landlords is not helped by those who continue to earn these negative stereotype labels. There are still slumlords, unfortunately, who take advantage of vulnerable tenants. Their apartments are poorly maintained, complaints are not answered, and communication is not attempted. These slumlords, however, provide insight into the baggage landlords have carried historically. Let's take a brief look.

A brief history of landlording

Ballad of the Landlord —Langston Hughes, 1940

My roof has sprung a leak.
Don't you 'member I told you about it
Way last week?

Landlord, landlord,
These steps is broken down.
When you come up yourself
It's a wonder you don't fall down.

Ten Bucks you say I owe you?
Ten Bucks you say is due?
Well, that's Ten Bucks more'n I'll pay you
Till you fix this house up new.

What? You gonna get eviction orders?
You gonna cut off my heat?
You gonna take my furniture and
Throw it in the street?

Um-huh! You talking high and mighty.
Talk on — till you get through.
You ain't gonna be able to say a word
If I land my fist on you.

Police! Police!
Come and get this man!
He's trying to ruin the government
And overturn the land!

Copper's whistle!
Patrol bell!
Arrest.

Precinct Station.
Iron cell.
Headlines in press:

MAN THREATENS LANDLORD

TENANT HELD NO BAIL

JUDGE GIVES NEGRO 90 DAYS
IN COUNTY JAIL.

Lords of the land

In medieval Europe (about 800 to 1200 A.D.), people were in constant danger from marauding bands of robbers and armies from other regions. In this context, castles and fortified towns were built and small armies were formed to defend the inhabitants of a region. The lords of the castles protected the small farmers in the surrounding land and villages, and, in return, the farmers paid the lord with a fixed portion of produce from their farms.

The Good Landlord

This barter system between the lord and the farmers, or "serfs," formed the basis of the landlord-tenant relationship we know today. There were several important differences: the "rent" consisted of food and the serf's house was considered to be his own. He was responsible for repairs. The lord owned only the land; hence the term "landlord."

It's easy to see that the power differential was very great between the lord and his serfs. Over the centuries, the system slowly evolved into renting houses and apartments, but this power differential remained much the same. The landlords were generally wealthy and the tenants poor. Legally, the landlords held all the power and often used this privilege to rent substandard housing and to evict tenants at will.

Progressive writers in the 19th century railed against the abuses of wealthy property owners. A favorite target was the absentee landlords in England who held vast tracts of land in Ireland. These landlords regarded the land and its impoverished inhabitants as simply a source of income from which to extract as much money as possible.

In the U.S., factory workers often lived in cramped, decaying tenements, and were exploited by greedy landlords because of the scarcity of housing. Landlords were able to evict tenants at will, and did. Melodramas and the popular press depicted these landlords as evil men dressed in black who took pleasure in putting widows and orphans out on the street. This was an exaggeration, of course, but one based in reality.

For centuries, therefore, landlords held a decisive advantage in legal, social, and economic power. They held the trump card: the virtually unchallenged right to evict. Charitable organizations such as churches and voluntary organizations dealt with poverty and homelessness. There was little tenants could do, if needed, to avoid being evicted.

Current challenges

We have come to a clear realization of the fact that true individual freedom cannot exist without economic security and independence…. We have accepted, so to speak, a second Bill of Rights under which a new basis of security and prosperity can be established for all—regardless of station, race, or creed. Among these are: the right to a useful and remunerative job… and the right of every family to a decent home….

—*President Franklin Delano Roosevelt, 1944*

After World War II, there was a sea change in public policy which profoundly shifted the balance of power between landlord and tenant. Government entered the housing market with major federal initiatives such as the **Housing Act of 1949** and the War on Poverty. To protect soldiers returning from World War II, city officials wrote the first municipal rent control statutes. By the 1960s, tenants found themselves with new bargaining powers. Laws enacted and court judgments at the national, state and city levels shifted from helping based on charity to an emphasis on rights. The most monumental of these was **Boston Housing Authority v. Hemingway**, which ushered in what is now referred to as the "warranty of habitability." This case set forth that all rental agreements must rest on

LEGAL INFO

The **Housing Act of 1949** was part of President Harry Truman's Fair Deal legislation. The purpose of the Act was to promote "urban renewal" by providing federal funds to tear down "slums" and build public housing; it also promoted home ownership by giving the Federal Housing Administration the power to provide mortgage insurance.

Boston Housing Authority v. Hemingway, 363 Mass. 184, 293 N.E.2d 831 (1973). This case held that a violation of the warranty of habitability means that the premises have conditions that endanger a tenant's health, safety, and well-being; and for a landlord to be held responsible for the violation, he must have knowledge of the condition in question.

the foundation of a "habitable," or livable, dwelling. Tenants were now able to withhold rent until repairs were done. When opinions differed about whether a repair was needed, the primary burden was now on the landlord to meet State standards.

Tenants also gained the right to sue for redress of discrimination, mishandling of security deposits, illegal access, and interference with utilities, among other wrongs. Although the legal framework pushed the landlords to new levels of accountability, it also changed the nature of the relationship by increasing each side's potential losses and fanning the flames of mistrust.

With the new laws and greater government involvement in the housing market, a new level of oversight emerged, together with a wide range of professionals to carry it out. These included social workers, case workers, housing search workers, inspectors, lawyers, mediators, advocates, and more. The responsibilities they were charged with—case management, advocacy, dispute resolution, inspection, enforcement, and others—were many and varied.

The landlord-tenant relationship, once negotiated between the parties themselves in relative privacy, was now carefully regulated. Contemporary laws now provided a firm set of ground rules, making both landlord and tenant accountable to external authorities. This gave tenants a range of recourses that could now be used as necessary defenses, but which could also sometimes be abused. Careful use of legal "protections" now enabled a tenant to mount a plausible threat of substantial losses if a landlord fought back.

As for landlords, although the world of rental property has changed radically in the last few decades, old stereotypes linger on. Outmoded images of landlords as greedy, selfish tyrants who hold all the power persist, aided and abetted by slumlords who still act as if they are not subject to the law. These perceptions can change over time, however, by more landlords using the practices outlined in this book. In addition to the personal satisfaction and increased success that will result, these practices can help you in another highly useful way—namely, to avoid expensive conflicts. These practices can help you create real win-win situations that will meet your business goals and make a difference. In the next chapter, we will discuss mistakes to avoid in order to make these practices work.

The Good Landlord

Questions for reflection:
Landlording in the 21st century

---

1. *Have you ever felt misunderstood as a landlord? Have you ever been stereotyped as a landlord? Please provide an example.*

_____
_____
_____
_____
_____

2. *What do you think are the roots of landlord stereotyping?*

_____
_____
_____
_____
_____

3. *What is it about landlording that may allow stereotyping to persist to this day?*

_____
_____
_____
_____
_____

4. *How has the landlord's power changed as a result of the rise in tenant's rights?*

_____
_____
_____
_____
_____

A Guide to Making a Profit While Making a Difference

4

Five common mistakes landlords make and how to avoid them

To err is human—but it can cost you dearly.

—Anonymous

Succeeding as a landlord means more than simply doing the right things; it also means avoiding the hazards inherent in the profession. I have undoubtedly made my own share of mistakes over my more than two decades as a landlord. Imagining a week in the life of a landlord can teach us about the risks.

A week in the life of a landlord

DAY 1: It's after 11 p.m. on a very cold night. Robin, my first floor tenant, just called, quite upset. There's no heat—again. I zip over to find her wrapped in a blanket; it's cold enough to see her breath. I do a simple diagnosis and discover that the thermocouple needs replacement again, the second time in a year. Robin is off to her friend's house, frustrated, and I have some emergency work to do.

DAY 2: Three rent checks arrive; there are six more outstanding. I get two e-mails that the "check's in the mail," which typically means another week. As long as I receive them by the 20th, I'll be all right. I e-mail the tenants to confirm their plans.

DAY 3: The cold snap is continuing. An ice dam has built up on the roof and is threatening to work its way down between the shingles and sheathing. There is a mammoth icicle that must be cracked off without damaging the exterior or injuring people below. I stop what I'm doing, get onto the roof with some tools, and hammer the massive block until it thunders to the ground.

The Good Landlord

Day 4: No landlord business except for a few checks coming in and some filing.

Day 5: A letter arrives from the local housing authority (LHA) which administers one of my tenant's Section 8 subsidies. The LHA is threatening to terminate her lease (which could lead to her rent subsidy being eliminated, causing me to have to evict her for nonpayment) because she hadn't completed her recertification requirements. I call the tenant and the LHA immediately to get the tenant to follow through.

Day 6: Another quiet day. Time to pay the mortgage and do some filing.

Day 7: I get a late afternoon call from a tenant who misplaced her key. She needs access. I'm on the other side of town but I get over to the property to let her in, for which I get enormous appreciation. While at her unit I discover some plumbing issues that need attention. I make a couple of temporary repairs, but then need to negotiate with three plumbers to secure one who can do the work tomorrow.

Later that evening, I get another call from an elderly tenant whose smoke detector has been going crazy. This detector is located right outside the kitchen—which is the right location, but prone to being set off accidentally. Worried about this tenant's cooking practices, I counsel the tenant on the phone.

These are just a few of the challenges landlords face every day. Given the complexities of the job, it's not surprising that landlords may fail to do some tasks correctly. In fact there are a number of mistakes that landlords may make which can cost them dearly. We don't have to look too far to appreciate the perils of landlording.

Introducing the five common mistakes

There are many mistakes that landlords can make. They can buy at the wrong time. They can hire the wrong contractor, underinsure the building, or fall behind on maintenance. The following, however, are five types of common mistakes that landlords can make in dealing with their tenants. Suggestions are included on how to avoid them.

1. Straying from the law

2. Losing your cool

3. Failing to communicate

4. Failing to establish a paper trail

5. Not using lawyers effectively

MISTAKE #1: Straying from the law

Scenario #1: When you requested a rent increase on the twenty-fourth of January, a week before February 1st when it would take effect, you assumed your tenant would be agreeable. You hadn't asked for a rent increase for over three years, and the amount was modest. You were shocked, however, when your tenant formally opposed it. The next day, in fact, your tenant sent you a certified letter with legal citations and references for what is required to raise the rent. You now had formal notification of requirements to follow. You also had new maintenance requests to respond to, and new restrictions on access, all because you asked your tenant for something not allowable by law. And you damaged your relationship with this tenant, which could be costly in a whole host of ways down the road.

Scenario #2: Personally, you've never felt comfortable with young people living together without being married. One day, however, you had your chance to put your values into action. You told a young couple that they couldn't rent your apartment because they weren't married. To your surprise, you got an outcry you never expected and a formal complaint letter as well! The letter from the prospective tenant seemed to come from outer space!

You assumed, innocently, that this was the kind of decision that a landlord could make without consequence. But here were the would-be tenants charging you with discrimination based on "marital status." They were asking for immediate access as new tenants to your apartment, or $2,500 in compensation! Suddenly, you needed to spend significant amounts of time and money to prepare your legal response. And then, if there was no resolution, the resulting proceedings would cost you further. And what if the matter didn't settle?

Suggestions: Acting without regard to the law can get you into hot water—and fast. You need to consider this, for example, before locking your tenants out without a judge's order. You need to consider the law as well before leaving a toilet unfixed indefinitely or refusing to rent to unmarried couples. These kinds of mistakes are avoidable and very expensive if you make them.

As a landlord, you are subject to quite a few *laws and regulations*—city, state, and federal. You need to know the laws that apply to your landlord business, and you need to follow them. At the same time, however, you want to keep your costs down whenever possible and maintain a cooperative relationship with your tenant.

Three steps to help you follow the law:

---

a. **Understand the landlord-tenant laws, policies, and regulations that apply to you.** *For example, a landlord cannot* **request a rent increase** *during the time period of a fixed-term lease. In Massachusetts, to request a rent increase, a landlord must provide notice of at least a one-month rental period or 30 days, whichever is longer. Not following these rules is not only illegal, but you'll also lose valuable tenant cooperation.*

b. **Understand your interests.** *Consider, for example, your desire to raise the rent without making necessary repairs. You know there are* **code-required** *(see page 66) repairs to be made, which can be costly. You can expect the tenant to push for these repairs depending upon how high a rent increase you request.*

To decide how much of a rent increase to request, you might want to consider how much the requested repairs may cost you in response. Although you are required by law to make only code-related repairs, you may end up making costly, non code-related repairs to satisfy tenant demands as well, all for a $20/month rent increase! I can remember more than one instance where I truly regretted my own decision to request a $20 rent increase, given the demands placed on me in response.

There are important reasons for pursuing rent increases whether or not repairs are requested by the tenant. Higher rents produce higher income, higher **cap rates** *(see page 66), and higher property resale vales. I am not suggesting that you avoid pursuing reasonable rent increases. Consideration for how your tenant will respond to the rent increase may affect what you charge, however. Earning less income now may secure valuable cooperation the next time you are in a conflict.*

Refer to The Good Landlord approach to eviction, page 186

c. **Assert your rights as well as your intention to satisfy your own and your tenant's interests.** *You can assert your rights by making threats and perhaps get a concession, but your tenant may be more likely to strike back the next time. Instead, as you assert your rights, why not also use a cooperative approach that can save you time and money while preserving your legal options.*

▦ LEGAL INFO: *REQUESTING A RENT INCREASE*

Check the laws in your own state regarding your options with a fixed term lease. In Massachusetts, a landlord cannot **request a rent increase** in the fixed-term lease even if the parties to a lease have agreed to the increase in writing. See Torrey v. Adams 254 Mass. 22, 27 N.E. 618 (1925). Under MGL Chapter 186, Section 12, the proper way to seek a rent increase is to give the tenant a 30-day notice (or usual rental period, whichever is longer). The reason for a fixed-term lease is to obligate the tenant for the term while at the same time preventing the landlord from increasing the rent during that term.

MISTAKE #2: Losing your cool

If you speak when angry, you'll make the best speech you'll ever regret.

—Groucho Marx

Maybe you've experienced this kind of problem: It's already the twenty-fourth of the month but no rent has appeared from a tenant who typically pays on time. You've phoned, sent e-mails and knocked on the door for over three weeks but no response. Now you're really mad. You have expenses too! You have to pay the mortgage, food, phone, and utility bills. **You need that rent!**

You call one final time before taking legal action. Unexpectedly she picks up the phone. Before you realize it, you're screaming at her, *"This is totally unacceptable! I cannot keep you as a tenant if you don't pay your rent on time! I don't want to have to chase you every month! I'm sick and tired of having to do it! I will evict you if you can't pay your rent on time! I have to pay bills too!"*

To your dismay, your tenant doesn't respond by apologizing or reaching for her pocketbook. Instead, you get back an earful: *"You don't realize what I've been going through the last few weeks with my job! I know I owe the money,*

■ **LEGAL INFO: *CODE REQUIREMENTS***

In Massachusetts, the state regulation of residential buildings is embodied in the State Sanitary Code, 105 Code of Massachusetts Regulations (CMR) 410.000 et seq. This code sets forth the minimum standards of fitness for human habitation.

DEFINITION: ***CAPITALIZATION RATE***

Capitalization rate (or "cap rate") is the ratio between the net operating income produced by an asset like a property, and the original price paid to buy the asset, or alternatively its current market value. The rate is calculated in a simple fashion as follows:

$$\text{CAPITALIZATION RATE} = \frac{\text{Annual net operating income}}{\text{Cost or value}}$$

but I don't need you to scream at me to make me pay it! And I'm not even talking about the two times last week you knocked on my door to make that repair before I was even dressed! You know it could have waited!"

Three days later you received your rent. You also received a stern letter detailing new limitations on access, four new repairs to be made, and a request to improve trash management. Your tenant also threatened to move out in two months unless you allowed her to include an additional tenant on the lease. Yes, you received the rent. You received an unexpected, major backlash as well.

Suggestions: Just when you are about to lash out, step back from the precipice to respond without getting angry or losing control. Consider whether lashing out will get you what you really want. Certainly, you want the rent. But don't you also want to make it most likely that your tenant will pay you on time the next month, and the month after that? You can always go the legal route. But why not make an extra effort to get what you want cooperatively before resorting to legal threats and costly court procedures?

We all know how easy it is to feel angry, particularly when we feel justified. Expressing your anger can be very effective in certain cases. There is a place for anger. For too many landlords, however, the heat rises and words they regret fly out before their better instincts remind them to cool down. When we lose control, we may destroy relationships and reduce cooperation just when it is most needed. It is possible to secure a late rent payment while also maintaining a good relationship with your tenant. The next time you need to negotiate but feel overwhelmed by anger, try the following:

Refer to Mindfulness, page 228

The Good Landlord

Four suggestions for dealing with anger:

---

a. Pause. *Do not make any decisions when you are angry. Before taking any action with your tenant, take four long, slow, deep breaths, or do whatever works for you to reduce your anger. You need to be able to think clearly before and during contact with your tenant. When you are calm and clear-headed, you will be in a better place to proceed.*

Refer to Mindfulness, page 228

b. Talk to someone, write it down, take a walk, or do anything that will allow your composure to return. *Find a friend, family member, neighbor, coworker, colleague, or anyone who has the time to hear you out and can give you his or her complete attention. Creating an opportunity to talk it out can make a huge difference. And sometimes the person you'll talk to will be yourself. Writing your thoughts and feelings in a journal or diary is another way to "talk things out."*

Refer to Emphasize warnings over threats, page 170

c. Prepare before you make contact with your tenant. *Consider how you want to have contact with your tenant. What form of communication will be best? You can try a more reasoned approach this time. The goal should be to get a workable agreement with your tenant without the use of threats.*

Refer to Prepare effectively—and make contact, page 134

d. Listen and learn. *When you speak with your tenant, your first task is to understand. Wait before telling your side of the story. Start with a question such as "What's your situation?" Then listen, and make sure she knows you've heard her. Only then should you tell your side of the story. Remember that listening to your tenant does not mean you need to agree with her. When your tenant feels acknowledged and understood, she will likely be more receptive and agreeable to your requests, including paying the rent!*

Refer to Seek to understand before being understood, page 147

SORRY FOR THAT OUTBURST EARLIER ... I KNOW ONCE IT COMES OUT, THERE'S NO WAY TO TAKE IT BACK ...

MISTAKE #3: Failing to communicate

It's been five days since Polly, a landlord I worked with, tried to secure access to her tenant's unit to make needed repairs. She had already purchased materials, lined up contractors, scheduled appointments, and tried every which way to reach the tenant, but received no response, not even a phone call. Last week her tenant was clamoring for repairs. This week Polly can't even find her! Polly spent a lot of time and money without anything to show for it, and now she's mad!

Failure to communicate can go both ways. Another landlord I worked with, George, received a list of needed repairs from his tenants, a couple with two young children. Two of the repairs were minor but one involved replacing a leaky hot water tank. When the couple didn't hear from George over the next three days, they felt they had no other choice but to call the building inspector. The inspector showed up immediately, citing a list of city code violations requiring urgent response. Then, still not hearing from George for two more days, the tenant made the next move, which was to threaten to withhold rent.

Even when communicating about repair issues is easy to do, many landlords simply don't do it. In this case, George was actually busy lining up a contractor to replace the hot water tank, but he didn't let the tenant know. This led the tenant to respond in an adversarial manner. Even if George had needed two or three more days to get things fixed, letting the tenant know could have made all the difference.

When problems, such as broken toilets, hot water, or heating systems need fixing immediately, tenants expect them to be addressed immediately. If they hear that you need time, and you follow up when you say you will, you can often buy that extra time—and flexibility as well. If, on the other hand, they do not hear from you, and the issues are urgent, they will undoubtedly assume the worst and raise the stakes. This can result not only in bad feelings between you and your tenants, but also significant added expense and stress.

You will succeed best by developing an effective communication system, one that has back-up procedures for when communication breaks down. Central to this system is your ability to regularly check your communication, whether you are using telephone, e-mail, text messages, Facebook, snail mail, face-to-face, or any other mode. It would serve you well to make a plan with your tenant for which mode(s) to use, and when. In addition, you need to make sure the tenant knows that you intend to fix things as soon as possible.

You want to establish yourself as the kind of person who cares about and responds in a timely fashion to your tenant's needs. The first few weeks and months of a tenancy is an important period of time for doing this. I try to be extra-responsive in addressing tenant concerns (even if they seem petty or annoying) during the first three months. The resulting positive relationship with your tenant can buy you flexibility when you most need it. It can also keep disputes from escalating if communication breaks down.

An example of a communication system you might use

a. **Decide in advance** *which communication format is best for a given situation. For some tenants, e-mail works best while for others texting may be better. Try to be flexible with each tenant's individual needs, in order to make communication easier. And remember, it is generally much better to have things in writing in order to establish a paper trail. For all follow-up communication, keeping a paper trail will be of enormous help if the case escalates.*

b. **Inform tenants** *about your intentions as early as you can. When you inform tenants early, you make it much easier to recruit them to your plan. Your tenants will appreciate the communication and be more likely to negotiate in good faith.*

c. **Follow up** *one or two more times if you don't hear from your tenants. Do not give up if you don't hear from them right away. Make the extra effort. Assume that your tenants want to speak with you and will respond if you are persistent. Try to reach them multiple times, and document your good-faith efforts.*

d. **Provide options** *for how to proceed whenever possible. There may be emergencies for which you need to move forward without offering options or agreeing to a plan. Whenever possible, however, you should give tenants choices regarding how to proceed. You will need to proceed without tenant input if you don't hear from them, but you will have given them options before you take action.*

e. **Confirm in writing** *any plans or agreements reached. When you do reach agreements or make a plan, your written confirmation will eliminate any confusion while also establishing a paper trail. Keep copies of any and all important communications that you have with your tenant.*

f. **Move forward** *even if your tenant doesn't respond to you, and continue to communicate. As indicated earlier, if your tenant does not respond, you will still need to move forward. But keeping tenants informed as you proceed can eliminate a great deal of potential trouble. It can also provide additional time for tenants to agree to the plan even if they are not enthusiastic about it. When working things out with tenants, it's better to communicate more than you think you need to than to communicate too little.*

MISTAKE #4: Failing to establish a paper trail

John has never liked handling the paperwork required of landlords, particularly when it comes to managing tenants. In addition, he just hasn't seen the value in keeping a record of every little thing. Now he is involved in a dispute with his tenant, Joan. In spite of multiple requests over a few tense days, he has failed to get her agreement to allow him access to fix a water leak, albeit a minor one, under her kitchen sink. Joan has had a different excuse each time. First, she had friends over. Another time she needed to get ready for something, and then she was just too busy. When pressed to allow access to make the repair, she insisted that she be present while workers were in her unit. No access date could be scheduled. When rent day came around, she paid her rent but continued to deny access.

Tensions began to escalate as John angrily insisted that he be given access. He was aware that the leak could cause the floor to rot if it wasn't fixed. In response, Joan filed more complaints, now over minor things like a few ants or a couple of loose tiles. Then John got a long document, detailing how he had mismanaged his maintenance and repair responsibilities.

At this point, John figured he had no choice but to go ahead with eviction based on denial of access. He got help preparing the right notices and applications. When trial day arrived, John went to court, confident that his case was strong and the judge would allow the eviction. In walked Joan, however, who stated to the judge that she had never been approached for access. John was stunned!

But when John was then asked for his documentation, he faced a large legal challenge. He had no paperwork to show for his efforts. It came down to his word against hers; and she claimed he had never told her that he was going to make the repair, had hired contractors, and wanted access. Without a paper trail, John couldn't show the judge his good faith efforts. Although John eventually got access to the unit, it took him much more time, money and stress than he ever could have imagined. And the eviction didn't happen!

As a property manager or landlord, you know the challenge: How can I be flexible and reasonable while protecting my rights? You might phrase it differently: "I want to be fair, but I don't want to be a sucker!"

Suggestions

a. ***Always put it in writing.*** It is important to communicate with tenants in writing and to establish a paper trail. Even if you communicate orally, you need to send a letter or e-mail—whichever mode you use with maximum success—confirming the conversation in writing. Because landlord-tenant disputes often turn on facts or interpretations that are presented differently by each party, things need to be spelled out precisely. Your written communication will serve as a formal record, a document you can submit to a judge. It will also serve as a reminder, whether months or years later, of what occurred. I find using e-mail to be very useful in this regard. E-mails create an automatic record of all interactions, including dates and times.

Establishing a paper trail prevents you from having to choose between the two extremes of being overly flexible versus pursuing eviction. A paper trail can help you reach workable agreements with your tenants while advancing your legal rights. In addition, should a disagreement end up

---

SOURCE: HOW TO LEAVE A PAPER TRAIL

The ideas in this section are credited to A. Joseph Ross, J.D., *How to Leave a Paper Trail: Record Keeping to Protect Yourself Financially and Legally* (Brookline, MA: Polaris Press, 2005).

In his publication *How to Be a Landlord and Avoid Legal Trouble* (Boston, MA: Law Office of A. Joseph Ross, J.D., 2015), Ross describes a case where "a tenant moved out, turned in the keys, left some property in the apartment, and then, a month or so later, wanted the apartment back. He brought suit in Housing Court, claiming that he had been illegally evicted, without judicial process. This could have been prevented by a paper trail, preferably something from the tenant in writing about his moving intentions. Failing that, the landlord might have written letters or e-mails to the tenant about the impending move or kept a record copy of a receipt given to the tenant for the keys he turned in."

in court, a paper trail can not only establish the facts of your case but also demonstrate your credibility. Documentation of your good faith efforts to work out agreements will make it easier to win your case if you end up in front of a judge.

Most importantly, establishing a paper trail can enable landlords to monitor progress toward agreements. Your paper trail can establish conditions to which the tenants can be held accountable.

b. **Create legible documents.** A central part of keeping a paper trail is to make sure any new documents are legible, and existing documents don't get marked up. Too often landlords write down phone numbers, descriptive information, or other notes on their documents. Courts want to see legible documents, preferably originals that are not marked up. If you must mark up a document, mark up a photocopy rather than the original. If you take pictures, don't write anything directly on the pictures. Keep your notes separate, on another print, or with an electronic copy of the picture. Jotting down your own notes on a document may make it inadmissible in court.

c. **Keep a rent ledger.** Your rent ledger should include which day the rent was received (not just the posting date), the check number, the amount collected, and the name of the account the check is drawn on or who paid

Consider the following situations that might require a paper trail:

- ❑ *"My tenant still hasn't put any garbage out on trash day and he's been living there for over two months."*

- ❑ *"My new tenant still owes the last month's rent, which he agreed to pay when we signed the* **lease**. *But he hasn't written or called."*

- ❑ *"My second floor tenant continues to disturb the peace of the other tenants."*

- ❑ *"The tenant has made multiple promises to pay the back rent but each time has not followed through."*

▨ LEGAL INFO: LEASE

Per Massachusetts General Law, a landlord can refuse to **lease** to a tenant if the tenant doesn't pay up front. However, in some cases, a landlord may accept a payment plan for the last month's rent, in which case such situations can occur.

the money. If a group of tenants sharing an apartment each pay separately, for example, your records should show the details for each check. In a dispute over rent, the winner will likely be the party whose records are better.

d. **Date each letter.** Date each letter and keep a copy. Save e-mails while dating them also, and back them up safely or print them out. If you deliver letters yourself by slipping them under the tenant's door, write down the date and time you did so on your own copy. You should also save all original correspondences you receive from the tenant, being sure to note on each document the date you received it.

e. **Follow up any direct communication with a written confirmation.** If you determine that a tenant is violating the lease, such as having unauthorized occupants, it is important to first contact the tenant to try to resolve the dispute. A letter should accompany your communication requesting that she or he cure the lease violation. If the violation goes uncorrected, you can state in the letter that unauthorized tenants are not allowed and that rent will be accepted without waiving your right to pursue eviction. If you don't state this, when you go to court and your tenant presents documentation that you accepted rent without reserving your rights while you knew of the lease violation, the judge can decide that you have waived your right to evict based on the lease violation in question.

f. **Keep hard copies.** It is still useful to keep hard copies of all correspondence. If you fax by computer, print out and save a hard copy of every fax with the transmission record. Judges have refused to admit a fax communication into evidence without a transmission record. If you use e-mail, remember to print out every e-mail received from or sent to each tenant, and save it. Because some e-mail software does not include identifying information on printouts, make sure that the header on the printout contains the basic information: to, from, subject, and date. You should write down any missing information on the printout when you print it out. If you keep electronic copies, which is recommended, be sure to regularly back up your data, using whatever medium–disc, hard drive, thumb drive, or web-based system–you prefer.

A casual, informal system of communicating and responding to tenant complaints is a lawsuit waiting to happen. You need to document, in an organized way, all rental payments, tenant complaints, work assignments, repairs made, and denial of access for repairs. Document your good faith efforts to handle any and all important tenancy issues. The more organized your records, the more credible will be your presentation before a court or administrative agency.

MISTAKE #5: Not using lawyers effectively

I'll pay $10,000 to a lawyer before I give one dollar to my tenant, the way she treated me!

—*Familiar landlord cry*

Almost every workday, this happens to me: a landlord calls, having heard that my program provides professional services for free. He wants a free attorney. Owed three, four or more months of back rent, this landlord is done. He wants to evict.

This landlord probably made some mistakes. He may not have established a paper trail. He may not yet have terminated the tenancy. There may be repairs needed in the unit and access is difficult. He may not have put the **security deposit** in a separate account. Although now he means business, and he's angry, he doesn't know what to do next. Using a medical metaphor, this landlord is losing blood and needs to stop the bleeding! He must protect his legal rights now.

When he approached a few attorneys, however, their fees were too high. Rather than paying $750, $1,000, $1,500, or more for an attorney to handle the case, he called me.

LEGAL INFO: *SECURITY DEPOSITS*

In Massachusetts, the rules for handling **security deposits** are very specific, and are governed by M.G.L. chapter 186 section 15B. Failure to follow the law precisely can result in the landlord forfeiting the deposit and even may expose him to treble (triple) damages under the Consumer Protection Act, Chapter 93A. (See page 199.)

Hiring an attorney to evict a tenant is often the right choice. An attorney may be the only person who can make contact with your tenant, when both of you are represented, by speaking with your tenant's attorney. An attorney can best help you prepare for trial when tenant defenses and counterclaims are extensive. There are plenty of times when attorneys are necessary.

An important judgment to make in managing tenants is when and how to involve professional help such as a lawyer or a mediator. Many landlords experience tension over the desire to be self-reliant and the recognition that using a lawyer can help avoid costly mistakes. When the mediation program I run is involved, for example, our housing attorney often does only a small piece of legal work at first. With legal assistance limited to drafting notices and responding to legal documents, the mediator or the landlord herself can handle most negotiations. Called *unbundling*, this concept of using a lawyer only for certain parts of the entire dispute resolution process has gained currency as an established legal practice.

Unbundling can often allow a landlord to reach agreements before court, through her own efforts, rather than to open herself up to the inevitable delays and legal twists and turns that accompany judicial decision-making. But if a landlord still ends up before the judge, unbundling does not prevent her from using an attorney for trial preparation and representation.

For example, you could employ a mediator to make a plan to gain access to make repairs, or to get the tenant to pay the back rent. A mediator can also coach you on how to rebuild trust, restore your tenant relationship, and improve future communication. Although a lawyer could also provide these services, many landlords may want to handle these issues themselves or

The Good Landlord

use **mediation** instead. A landlord or tenant could also use a process called **collaborative law**.

Whether the rent is past due a couple weeks or five months, professional legal assistance can make a big difference. You may have questions about repairs, access, noise and nuisance, property damage, subletting, pets, rent increases, and much more, for which an attorney can provide invaluable help. The question is: for which parts of your case with your tenants do you need an attorney? When you need to keep costs down, improve your tenant relationships, and secure future cooperation:

1. ***Remember you may be purchasing services by the hour.*** You will spend the same amount per hour whether your attorney drafts documents, calls to remind you to follow up with your tenant, or sends whatever documents you request. Organize yourself carefully so that the time for which your lawyer bills you is for legal services, not logistical details. Use your lawyer's time wisely, so that the time for which your lawyer bills you is for legal services, not logistical details.

DEFINITION: MEDIATION

"The common denominator of all ADR [Alternative Dispute Resolution] methods is that they are faster, less formalistic, less expensive, and often less adversarial than a court trial.... **Mediation** [is] a way that parties can resolve their own dispute without going to court. In mediation, a neutral third party (the mediator) meets with the opposing sides to help them find a mutually satisfactory solution. Unlike a judge or an arbitrator, the mediator has no power to impose a solution—instead, the mediator facilitates the parties' communication and helps to develop and reality-test possible solutions. No formal rules of evidence or procedure control mediation; the mediator and the parties usually agree on their own informal ways to proceed..." (The editors of Nolo and Gerald and Kathleen Hill, *Nolo's Plain-English Law Dictionary*, Berkeley, CA: Nolo, 2009, 21, 268.) Mediation is commonly used in divorce cases and in real estate and business disputes.

DEFINITION: COLLABORATIVE LAW

Collaborative law is a new dispute resolution model in which both parties to the dispute retain separate lawyers whose only job is to help them settle the dispute. If the lawyers do not succeed in helping the clients resolve the problem, the lawyers must withdraw from the case and can never again represent either client against the other. All participants agree to work together respectfully, honestly, and in good faith to try to find "win-win" solutions that satisfy both parties. No one may go to court, or even threaten to do so, and if that should occur, the collaborative law process terminates and both lawyers are disqualified from any further involvement in the case. Lawyers hired for a collaborative law representation can never under any circumstances go to court for the clients who retained them.

2. ***Plan ahead.*** All of us would prefer an attorney who is inexpensive, quick and effective. Unfortunately, you may not always get all three of these. You can reduce costs while maintaining quality, however, by planning ahead. Instead of giving your lawyer his assignment the day before it is due, when the pressure is on and quality and thoroughness may be compromised, give him his assignment as early as possible.

3. ***Carefully assess the effect that escalating your case may have.*** Although your lawyer may be preparing you for trial without any chance to turn back, you may want to slow things down, negotiate more, and pursue resolution yourself. While your lawyer is cautioning you to pursue settlement talks, on the other hand, you may feel headstrong about going to the judge. Assessing whether or not to keep escalating your case is a very important step, and needs to be done very carefully. Although your own sensibilities can make for good assessment, I urge you to consult the professionals you hire, along with knowledgeable and trustworthy friends and family members.

4. ***Consider unbundling your legal services.*** Unbundling legal services is a practice in which the lawyer will provide some, but not all, of the work involved in traditional, full-service legal representation. Clients choose the legal assistance according to their own needs and do the remaining tasks themselves. For example, a lawyer could advise you about the law, judicial process, and negotiation strategies, and draft documents, but leave the tenant negotiations to you. You could do the court filings, submit your **Answer** and **Request for Discovery** and handle negotiations yourself, but have a lawyer represent you in court. There are three general approaches to consider:

   Attorney as Coach: Your attorney advises on the law and how to resolve the dispute, without formally representing you. Coached

---

LEGAL INFO: ANSWER AND REQUEST FOR DISCOVERY

In Massachusetts, after a tenant has been served with a Summons and Complaint, the tenant may file an **Answer** and **Request for Discovery** from the landlord, but this legal paperwork must reach the landlord and the court by the Monday before the scheduled trial date. An Answer may consist of any denials of whatever statements the landlord made in his complaint, as well as counterclaims the tenant may have against the landlord. Discovery includes asking the landlord to answer written questions (Interrogatories) as well as asking the landlord to produce specific documents related to the tenancy. If the Answer includes a Request for Discovery, the trial date automatically gets extended to two weeks after the original date. (See Massachusetts Rules of Court, Uniform Summary Process Rules, Rules 3, 5 and 7.) For this reason, tenants may use this as a delaying tactic even if they actually do not want the information requested in the Request for Discovery. Landlords may file a Request for Discovery from tenants. Go to page 178 for a discussion of defenses and counterclaims.

by your attorney, you produce your own notices and documents, submit your Answer and Request for Discovery, and negotiate. You maintain control as you pursue settlement before going to court.

Attorney as Coach and Document Producer: Your attorney coaches while also drafting legal notices and documents, submitting the Answer and Request for Discovery, and preparing for trial. You stay involved with negotiations, albeit closely assisted.

Attorney for complete service: Your attorney handles production of all notices and documents, submission of Answer and Request for Discovery, pre-trial negotiations, trial preparation and representation on trial day—the entire case.

In this chapter, I've discussed five common mistakes—*straying from the law, losing your cool, failing to communicate, failing to establish a paper trail,* and *not using lawyers effectively*—and how to avoid them. Of course there are many more possible mistakes that landlords can make. I know this all too well from my own experience. The five presented here, though, stem from problems in dealing with people. And that's what much of this book is about: helping you avoid costly mistakes while establishing the most effective approach to managing your tenants. Avoiding these costly mistakes will allow you to meet your tenant's interests when it is in your interest to do so, rather than as a result of your missteps.

Questions for reflection: Five common mistakes landlords make and how to avoid them

---

1. What is a typical day-in-the-life like for you as a landlord? Give an example of one or two days: _____

   _____

   _____

2. Have you as a landlord ever made any of these key mistakes? If so, give an example, and reflect on what you learned.

   a. Not following the law: _____

   _____

   _____

   b. Losing your cool: _____

   _____

   _____

   c. Failing to communicate: _____

   _____

   _____

   d. Failing to establish a paper trail: _____

   _____

   _____

   e. Not using lawyers effectively: _____

   _____

   _____

3. What would it be like to follow the suggestions in this book? Do you agree with these suggestions? _____

   _____

   _____

5 Beyond the bottom line:
Why landlords help

*[There is] a remarkable distinction between justice
and all the other social virtues . . . The practice of
friendship, charity, or generosity seems to be left
in some measure to our own choice, but. . .we feel
ourselves to be in a peculiar manner tied, bound,
and obliged to the observation of justice.*

—Adam Smith

There are two strong democratic traditions that weave through our history as Americans: individualism and civic engagement. America was founded in the tradition of civic engagement: indeed, the American Revolution represented a large group of diverse people fighting together for economic and political freedom. Individualism was also established early on, and continues to this day.

Lessons learned from these traditions can offer invaluable insights into how landlords can make a profit while making a difference. Let's discuss these two traditions further and explore what meaning they provide for landlords.

Early American democracy

Alexis de Tocqueville (see page 84), a French sociologist, observed these two traditions in early American democracy as a vibrant part of the foundation for our new country. For example, he observed that being successful at one's job often depended on one's involvement in civic life. When a local shoemaker helped organize a town parade and a clothing drive as well, for example, the fellow townspeople's respect for that shoemaker

---

DEFINITION: **CIVIC ENGAGEMENT**

Civic engagement can be defined as individual and collective action designed to identify and address issues of public concern. Civic engagement can take many forms— from individual volunteerism to organizational involvement to electoral participation. It can include efforts to address an issue directly, to work with others in a community to solve a problem, or to interact with the institutions of representative democracy.

The Good Landlord

would increase; and more townspeople would patronize the shoemaker's business. People thrived through being civic-minded as business owners, family members, and as active participants in the community. They understood it to be their civic duty to engage publicly on the issues of the day which could help not only their communities but their own bottom lines as well.

Noting how individualism was taking root, however, Tocqueville expressed concern. Tocqueville observed "more and more people who, though neither rich nor powerful enough to have much hold over others, have acquired enough wealth to be able to look after their own needs. Such folk owe no man anything and hardly expect anything from anybody. They form the habit of thinking of themselves in isolation."

Tocqueville was observing the growth of American individualism, a quality that was closely tied to the opportunity to acquire wealth. Individual Americans wished to acquire large fortunes for themselves, and believed they could accomplish this through hard work and determination. Tocqueville perceived a profound difference between American and European values; whereas most people in the European lower classes held out little hope of dramatically improving their lot, many in America's lower classes felt very hopeful of doing so.

In place of the ethic of frugality and austerity that once ruled American life, Tocqueville observed, many Americans were no longer denying themselves anything, upholding the principle that "I have a duty to myself." An individual might now choose to buy eggs from a farmer a few towns

---

HISTORICAL BACKGROUND: ALEXIS DE TOQUEVILLE

Alexis de Tocqueville, born in 1805, was a French political thinker and historian best known for *Democracy in America* (two volumes, 1835 and 1840) and *The Old Regime and the Revolution* (1856). In both of these works, he explored the effects of the rising equality of social conditions on the individual and the state in Western societies. *Democracy in America*, his major work, published after his travels in the United States, is today considered an early work of sociology and political science.

over because of a slight break in price, despite the fact that his next door neighbor, whose eggs he had been buying, was a local volunteer firefighter and active town meeting member. Private interests began to take precedence over community interests.

Individualism and civic engagement in the 21st century

Fast forward to the 21st century. New research confirms what Tocqueville raised as a concern early on. This research reveals what many of us may have experienced but not necessarily acknowledged. Take Robert Putnam's conclusions in **Bowling Alone**. Putnam observed a dramatic decrease in the numbers of people joining associations of any kind, even bowling leagues. From 1975 to 2000, Putnam points out, sharp declines occurred in social interactions such as attending club meetings (down 58%) and having friends over (down 35%). In civic life, Putnam also observed the same phenomenon of decreasing involvement.

Citing a wide span of research documenting decreasing social interaction across different strata of American society, Putnam and other researchers came to a sobering conclusion: the newly developing American individualism and the isolation that results have been on the rise and have, in fact, increased Americans' feelings of loneliness and depression. The research indicates that, without a sense of connection, creative expression,

---

SOURCE: BOWLING ALONE

In *Bowling Alone: The Collapse and Revival of American Community* (New York: Simon & Schuster, 2000), Robert D. Putnam surveys the decline of "social capital" in the United States of America since 1950. He describes the reduction in all the forms of in-person social intercourse used by Americans to educate themselves and enrich the fabric of their social lives. He believes this loss of social contact undermines the active civic engagement a strong democracy requires of its citizens. Putnam discusses ways in which Americans have disengaged from political involvement including decreased voter turnout, public meeting attendance, serving on committees, and working with political parties.

or commitment to people or things beyond oneself, daily routines may not contribute to a sense of personal fulfillment and happiness. The yearning to find meaning and happiness in daily life, whether at work or in social interactions, is going unfulfilled for many.

Interestingly enough, the September 11 terrorist attack is one example of how such patterns of isolation and resulting unhappiness can change. In the aftermath of the attacks, many individuals reported awakening to a sense of higher purpose. After the tragedies of that day, some began to gain a new perspective on their lives. They became inspired to pursue personal dreams and find new meaning for themselves as members of their families and communities.

This is part of a trend that runs counter to the theme of *Bowling Alone*. In **Blessed Unrest**, Paul Hawken describes the growing number of groups concerned with social justice, helping the underprivileged, or protecting the environment. From billion-dollar non-profits to tiny dot.com causes, these groups include millions of engaged people in this country and around the world. Hawken terms it "the largest collective movement on Earth."

In the same vein, research confirms the individual benefits that come from the practice of being helpful, also known as **helper's high**. "Helper's high is pretty simple," says Stephen G. Post, Professor of Preventive Medicine and

---

SOURCE: *BLESSED UNREST*

In *Blessed Unrest: How the Largest Movement in the World Came into Being and Why No One Saw It Coming* (New York: Viking Press, 2007), Hawken argues that a vast world-changing "movement with no name" is now forming, which he believes will prevail. He conceives of this movement as developing not by ideology but rather through the identification of what is and is not humane.

DEFINITION: *HELPER'S HIGH*

Helper's high is a term coined by psychologists to describe a euphoric feeling followed by a longer period of calm, experienced after performing a kind act. It is often referred to as a positive addiction and related to the economic concept of "warm-glow giving." The physical sensation results from the release of endorphins, and is followed by a longer-lasting period of improved emotional well-being and sense of self-worth, feelings that in turn reduce stress and improve the health of the helper.

Founding Director of the Center for Medical Humanities, Compassionate Care, and Bioethics at Stony Brook University School of Medicine. "To rid yourself of negative emotional states," he said, "you need to push them aside with positive emotional states and the simplest way to do that is to just go out and lend a helping hand to somebody."

According to a Gallup Poll, nearly 90% of Americans give money to charitable causes on a yearly basis and 62% have volunteered for a charity in the past year. Gallup's Annual Lifestyle Survey, conducted Dec. 5–8, 2005, also found that one in seven Americans say they have donated blood in the past year. In another study, 83% of blood donors indicated a willingness to undergo anesthesia and stay overnight in a hospital to donate bone marrow to a complete stranger.

What these studies demonstrate moves us beyond the bleak reports of Tocqueville and Putnam. Despite the compelling tugs of individualism in today's world, many people are meaningfully pursuing their community's interests as well as their own interests. More and more people are discovering in today's world how they literally can *increase their personal happiness by helping their neighbors, friends, fellow countrymen, and the international community*. Although in this book we discuss "helping" as meeting a landlord's enlightened self-interests, as being a good or even a super-good landlord, this dimension of helping can take on a life of its own. Being helpful can be healing to the world. It can be healing, as well, to oneself.

Helping as a landlord

Everyone can give something.

—President Bill Clinton

What does all this mean for life as a landlord? Over several decades since 1945, as we learned in Chapter 3, legislation was passed that increased tenants' rights. The newly codified laws pushed landlords to become publicly accountable for things previously done from a sense of duty. As many Americans found their peace through acts of helping, many landlords have done the same. And because landlords by nature truly depend upon the communities where their properties lie, there are always examples of how they can be helpful.

Communities of which landlords are a part include:

- ❒ *Landlord associations*
- ❒ *Landlords and tenants*
- ❒ *Landlords and contractors, suppliers and other business people*
- ❒ *Landlords and their families, estate beneficiaries, and others who will inherit their property*
- ❒ *Landlords and their neighbors*

Motivated by the benefits from engaging these communities, many landlords have extended a helping hand to tenants in distress. Many landlords have also enhanced the features of their properties, volunteered for causes they care about, contributed to neighborhood improvement activities, joined national or international nonprofit groups, and more.

Of course, being a successful landlord, whether good or super-good, depends on making money. Whatever positive effects a landlord can have, whether beautifying the building, volunteering time, or "working with" tenants in need, she can do these things because she is making money. Equity, resale, and monthly cash flow all generate income. And when landlords are making money, they can consider whether or how to give back.

More than money

There are times, however, landlords report, when they are motivated by more than money. Beyond meeting merely their enlightened self-interests, these landlords, who I have named "super-good" in this book, go further. Although for most landlords such practices are not possible due to finances, time, or personal choice, there are many super-good landlords who do these practices every day and thrive. These super-good landlords are a force for social good.

In some cases, I caution, such attempts to do super-good landlord practices, let alone meet your enlightened self-interests, can backfire. Be careful! Landlords should not continue doing these practices without a clear sense of how to be effective. We'll see, in the next chapter when I discuss the *helping trap*, what mistakes are possible.

In any situation where a landlord helps a tenant, there is always the possibility that the landlord's efforts will fail and he will lose even more money. But in spite of this possibility, super-good landlords continue to be helpful to tenants.

The Good Landlord

Three examples of super-good landlord practices

---

1. ***After three years of paying the rent on time,*** *a single mom with two kids loses her job and falls behind. Her landlord carries her for four months without rent, helping her out with babysitting, researching job leads, filling out forms, and shopping. When the tenant finally finds a job, the landlord forgives two months' rent and accepts a payment plan for the rest.*

2. ***A long-term tenant who is elderly and disabled faces significant health costs*** *that make him unable to pay the rent for some time. After appealing to the tenant's family, who the landlord has known for many years, the landlord determines that he can only get eight out of the twelve months that are owed. Knowing that he has done well enough over the years and can expect to recoup his losses, the landlord agrees to forgo the lost rent and maintain the tenancy.*

3. ***A young couple with three young children falls upon hard times.*** *The husband loses his job and the wife can only work part-time due to her child-raising responsibilities. Family tensions flare up over financial issues, but when eviction and possible homelessness become an issue, the family appeals to the landlord for help. Having cultivated appreciation and respect for these tenants, the landlord agrees to work with them. He exchanges five months' back rent for barter. The plan is conditioned on the following:*

   A. *The husband agrees to pursue his own carpentry business (keeping a daily log to document his progress).*

   B. *The couple agrees to do ongoing property maintenance (enough hours to pay for the five months of back rent). The landlord can terminate the agreement at any time if quality and timeliness of work aren't sufficient.*

   C. *The tenants keep the yard and basement clean.*

   D. *They restore peace to the premises (i.e., no more fighting) .*

Motivation

Let's look at what motivates these landlords. First of all, when you get to know and appreciate a tenant and her family, for example, and you see them suffer, it can be hard to remain neutral. You may have developed a strong, positive relationship with this family. On some important level you care about them. This increases your motivation to help.

As a landlord, furthermore, you are uniquely positioned to understand the risk of homelessness faced by this family. Because you are in the business of providing housing, you can understand the pain and anxiety of their situation. They may have no safety net—no family members, friends, or savings—nothing to fall back on if evicted.

The compassion you feel may become even stronger when you realize you have the potential to make a tremendous difference in the lives of these family members. You can make it possible for this family to have a home.

Being helpful to tenants who are experiencing great difficulties may be viewed as just good business practice or simple human decency. But landlords may feel compelled to do so even when it is not prudent. We see this type of generosity practiced by many landlords, no matter how inconvenient it may be.

In the real world, people routinely extend their help and experience helpers' high in the process, even when a competing internal voice tells them to bar the door and guard the checkbook! Landlords make real sacrifices and can, in the process, make an enormous difference for their tenants. Tenants often respond by taking good care of their units and doing favors in return. A sense of community is created and everyone benefits.

The Good Landlord

Landlords mention these rewards for being helpful to others while contributing to the common good

---

Feeling better about oneself

Feeling more personally powerful, less afraid

Pride in accomplishment

Satisfaction in helping, in making a contribution, in doing one's share, in making the world more like it "should be"—more fair, caring, etc.—more consistent with one's values

Feeling better physically

More energy

Greater calm

More overall sense of happiness and well-being

Meaningful relationships

Feelings of mutual respect and caring for those with whom you interact

Learning

Better communication skills

Wisdom: discovering the difference between what is meaningful and what is trivial.

More insight into oneself

Satisfaction in expressing care for those we get to know well and care about

Knowing that one's efforts will create a better future for those we care about

Mentoring

Seeing those you've "helped" or "coached" grow and succeed

Being able to give to others

Recognition

Respect from others

Appreciation

Public visibility

Sense of purpose in life, improved hope

A framework with which to make sense of the world

Understanding how one's individual efforts can contribute to advancing the common good

Material improvements in the quality of life

Better housing, neighborhood, environment, etc.

INFORMATION REFERENCE

This chart is adapted from Frances Moore Lappé and Paul Martin Du Bois, *The Quickening of America: Rebuilding Our Nation, Remaking Our Lives* (San Francisco: Jossey-Bass, 1994).

Helping as a balancing act

As we can see, this interdependence gives both landlords and tenants a tremendous potential to be responsible and genuinely helpful to each other. But this potential brings its own set of questions:

- How much generosity is appropriate and productive in a landlord-tenant relationship?
- How much flexibility is appropriate in a landlord-tenant relationship? In what ways do our own acts of flexibility help to stabilize tenancies? How might our own actions help to destabilize tenancies?
- What kinds of responsible behavior should we expect from tenants as part of this bargain?
- How can we distinguish between helpfulness that inspires a positive response and helpfulness that furthers dependency? How might this dependency lead tenants and landlords to avoid addressing more significant problems?

These are the kinds of questions that landlords need to consider. The impulse to do good in an unselfish manner is one of the highest expressions of human nature. But in the landlord-tenant relationship, this impulse needs to be tempered with caution. Finding a balance between your desire to help and your personal constraints, as dictated by money, time, and individual choice, is essential for success.

In the next chapter, we'll discuss one of the most difficult challenges: the helping trap. A helping trap can occur when, after a tenant fails to respond to your helping efforts, she turns against you. We'll talk about actions that can lead to helping traps and how they may compromise your success as a landlord. The chapters that follow this will then discuss how to avoid falling into such a trap.

How can you, as a good or super-good landlord, maximize success, given the other interests involved?

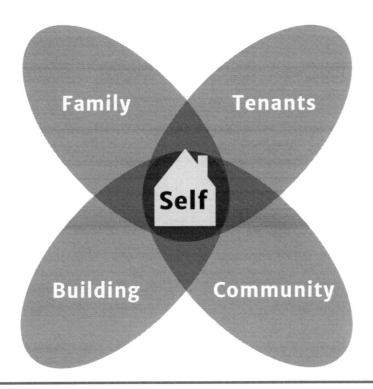

**Questions for reflection: Beyond the bottom line:
Why landlords help**

---

1. *How do you provide "help" to others in your daily life? In what ways might
you have "helped" your tenants? Provide an example. Do you ever think of
how you manage tenants as being "helpful"?*

_____

_____

_____

_____

_____

_____

2. *What is it about being a landlord that may inspire this helping orientation?
How may your helping orientation as a landlord interfere with your need to
make a profit?*

_____

_____

_____

_____

_____

_____

3. *How might your helping orientation improve your bottom line? Support your
tenants? Support your neighborhood?*

_____

_____

_____

_____

_____

_____

6 When helping your tenant hurts you:
The helping trap

If I knew for a certainty that a man was coming to my house with the conscious design of doing me good, I should run for my life.

—Henry David Thoreau

I liked the guy. I trusted him when he told me he would pay his back rent. Now it's been five months.

—Cambridge, Massachusetts Landlord

I've been watching Sandy and her three kids struggling for months. How could I evict her knowing her predicament? So I worked with Sandy...and worked with her and on and on until it became seven months without rent, and when I finally spoke up, the next call was from her lawyer!

—*Malden, Massachusetts Landlord*

In the previous chapter, we discussed why landlords help, why it feels good to do so, and how it can occur naturally. In offering help, however, it is necessary to exercise some care; otherwise, you could fall into what I call the "helping trap." A helping trap is a situation where you try to lend a hand but you wind up getting hurt. In this chapter, we'll discuss what a helping trap looks like, how much emotional stress and cost is involved, and how hard it can be to prevent it from happening. Let's start by discussing an unfortunate landlord saga involving a young couple I worked with who, despite their good intentions, fell into the helping trap.

Joe and Maria's story

Joe and Maria, owners of a four-family building, are typical small landlords. "Our vision was to be able to buy a piece of real estate, fix it up, move in, and find good tenants," said Joe. "We loved the sense of community and the chance to provide affordable housing while making a reasonable income."

After they bought the building, Joe had a chance to put his carpentry skills to good use. The diversity of tenants they inherited in the building was also exciting to both of them. Brenda and Sam, a young couple with two kids, were among the new tenants Joe and Maria liked the most. The couple loved the apartment's charm, and seemed to ignore its disrepair. Joe and Maria realized that the unit needed quite a few improvements: a new tile floor in the kitchen, sanding and sealing the hardwood floors, remodeling in the bathroom, some new windows, and a back door. They expected to finance these improvements, amounting to about $5,000, over time from the rental income.

Brenda and Sam, however, had a different idea. "Please don't go to all that trouble," said Sam. "The apartment is fine as it is, and the absolute top dollar we can afford is $750 a month." For Joe and Maria, this was a new perspective on doing good, introduced by the very people they wanted to help. They could keep the rent below market and avoid the costly renovations. They would let their tenants' needs and priorities take precedence over their renovation plan.

Everyone signed the lease with a feeling of real optimism, and everything seemed to go well for the first few months. Small favors were exchanged, like doing some food shopping for each other and working together on a vegetable garden.

"It was a moral decision for us," said Joe, looking back on what happened. "We didn't want to behave like typical gentrifiers, pricing the apartment out of reach of ordinary people. We wanted our apartment to be habitable, safe and affordable as well. We wanted to be different."

Joe and Maria were very pleased with the arrangement. However, after a few months, Sam's hours at the local tree service company were cut by one-third. At first, he made up the money by working odd jobs as a carpenter. But, in spite of this, the family income gradually deteriorated, and soon, so did their behavior. Suddenly, there were kids banging and yelling, day or night. Loud arguments between the adults also broke out, and these prompted several police visits. The neighbors began to complain. Growing numbers of empty beer bottles were set out for recycling. And Brenda and Sam fell behind in their rent.

Maria and Joe watched and waited, growing increasingly uncomfortable and angry. Eventually, they spoke to the tenants, who were apologetic and hopeful, which prompted Maria and Joe to be patient for some time regarding rent collection. Promises were made, but there were more incidents, and then more promises, but no rent.

By the time Brenda and Sam owed six months rent, Maria and Joe were done trying to work it out. Finally, after another two weeks elapsed, Joe and Maria started eviction proceedings. The case seemed clear. There were witnesses aplenty to confirm their testimony of property damage and nuisance behavior in addition to the back rent.

However, three days before the eviction trial day, Joe and Maria received legal documents, signed by a lawyer. And the trial date was automatically extended for two weeks. According to the lawyer, Brenda and Sam were now "rent withholding." A building department report was enclosed, citing code violations based on the very problems the tenants had asked Joe and

Refer to Rent abatements, page 9

Maria not to fix! Brenda and Sam were now demanding thousands of dollars in rent abatements based on state law, dating back to the move-in. Joe and Maria were also charged with illegal access, harassment, retaliation, and a host of other allegations (which the tenants had never complained about). And, the lawyer stated, Maria and Joe couldn't even speak to the tenants! Everything had to go through the lawyer.

As you can imagine, Joe and Maria felt profoundly confused and betrayed. Not in their wildest dreams had they ever imagined this kind of treatment. The relationship they had developed with these tenants led them to expect cooperation not just in good times, but in difficult times too. In addition to choosing not to gentrify, Joe and Maria had sacrificed income to accommodate a family in need. But when Joe and Maria finally believed it fair to proceed with legal eviction, their tenants became highly resistant and combative to Joe and Maria's plan.

Perhaps you've experienced some version of this episode, with all the possible feelings of shock, anger, despair, and revenge. You may have discovered, to your dismay, how time-consuming, expensive, adversarial, and downright difficult it can be to work with these situations. Whether they come about from your tenants' legitimate needs or from their hidden agendas, these situations can trigger a profound desire to retaliate. Conflicts like these can suck the life energy out of you, leaving you cynical, revengeful, and ready to quit the business altogether. For over twenty years, in fact, I've watched many landlords lose their interest in, and even leave, the landlording business because of circumstances like these.

Damned if you do, damned if you don't

As a landlord you know the challenge: how can you be reasonable with your tenants while protecting your rights? You might phrase it differently when you are with your friends: "I want to be fair but not be a sucker!" Both statements sum up the same problem.

The kind of situation illustrated by Joe and Maria's story presents an enormous trap for landlords. It can be very difficult to pursue legal procedures against a nonpaying tenant, particularly if they're at risk of homelessness. You don't want to be the reason why someone loses their home let alone becomes homeless. Thus it is natural to be patient with a tenant who "needs some time" to pay the back rent. And most tenants expect you to be patient if all they need is time. But how much time? The need to avoid homelessness can motivate many tenants to push you past the limits of your patience, which can be self-fulfilling for landlords not wanting to be perceived as scrooges. This sets the stage for tremendous rent losses if tenants ultimately cannot pay the back rent for months before landlords take legal action.

FIRST, DEACTIVATE THE TRAPS...
SECOND, FREE CHEESE EVERY MORNING AT EIGHT...
THIRD, LOSE THE CAT...
FOURTH, FREE CHEESE EVERY NIGHT AT SIX...

BRIAN NEGOTIATES FOR HIS TV REMOTE

What if you keep the rent low but the tenant still cannot pay? Communication has broken down. You throw your hands up and decide to "go legal." You serve an eviction notice. But then you hear back. You get an inspection report of the unit from the local building department. Your tenant denies you access to make needed repairs. Your tenant demands her security deposit be returned, alleging you've mishandled it. You smell the makings of a full legal defense. You face the legal costs, countless hours of prep time, and the emotional stress of having to fight against a tenant with whom you have been patient and flexible, and to whom you have extended a helping hand! And you have lost lots of money!

Joe and Maria certainly learned one important lesson, in perhaps the most painful way possible. That is, in whatever way they may have exchanged lower rents for keeping costs down, they will still be held to the highest legal standard if they face a fight over eviction. Avoiding spending money on maintenance and repair, as Joe and Maria did, can be a recipe for legal disaster.

Beyond codependency as a landlord

We've seen how Joe and Maria tried to be helpful by setting up an exchange, that is, receiving below-market rents in exchange for low overhead.

I've heard from numerous landlords how seeing vulnerable tenants motivates their desire to help. The sight of a low-income single mom struggling to get her kids off to school, knowing she is doing whatever she can to provide for her family, inspires **compassion**. Whether it is offering a ride, a grocery run, or patience with the rent, helping such tenants to avoid homelessness is a unique contribution that landlords can make. Think about it: no other individual is able to meet such a basic need as providing a home for tenants at such a vulnerable moment! Many landlords tell me that they experience great satisfaction from performing such an important act.

Compassion, whether for a friend in need or for a tenant who is struggling, encourages one to help out. Providing too much help with no clear **boundaries**, however, can become a problem. Many landlords I've worked with will extend extra months of credit with only modest hope of

---

DEFINITION: *COMPASSION*

Compassion is "sympathetic consciousness of others' distress together with a desire to alleviate it." (*Webster's Online Dictionary*)

DEFINITION: *BOUNDARY*

A **boundary** is "something that indicates or fixes a limit or extent" (*Merriam-Webster.com*). Ideally, one develops flexible boundaries.

being paid. And when past due payments pile up for too many months, unfortunately many tenants will not be able to make up the gap, even with outside assistance.

In cases like these, a landlord's compassion may turn into codependency—that is, making the tenant more dependent on the landlord and causing the relationship to deteriorate. By the time the landlord does pull back, he may already be very resentful and full of revenge. These feelings will surely escalate if the tenant mounts a legal defense.

Here is the kind of complaint I often hear from landlords: "How could she turn against me now? After I waited patiently for months without having received rent, while having allowed extra roommates, taken her kids to daycare, researched job leads, and overlooked the property damage—after all that, when I finally took legal action, she then mounted a legal defense! I feel so betrayed!"

Is it possible for landlords to avoid this experience? As landlords make a profit, can they also be helpful without becoming victims of their own good intentions? Understanding what **codependency** (see page 104) means can help.

Finding a balance

Being a landlord offers the potential to express much generosity—and make a profit—without becoming codependent. Landlords, uniquely, can be helpful while still pursuing their own interests. Many landlords, whether or not they recognize it, balance financial gains with the capacity to do good for tenants, the neighborhood, and the world. "Balance" is the operative word here. Learning to balance the pull between self-interests and other interests is the key to success.

The Good Landlord

In Chapter 5, we discussed the great satisfaction that lending a helping hand can bring. In this chapter, we raised the specter of the helping trap—offering too much help without setting good boundaries, thereby becoming a victim of your own compassion. This helping trap can destroy the landlord-tenant relationship, causing great financial and emotional pain to both parties.

Looking ahead

In the following chapters, you will discover strategies for finding a balance between flexibility and self-interest. Instead of being too helpful in certain instances, running the risk of getting burned, you will learn how to pursue your enlightened self-interests. You'll learn how to avoid "going legal" in certain instances. You'll also learn how to assess when eviction should be pursued. And you will learn how to pursue eviction when you need to, and how to do so without escalating the dispute unless absolutely necessary.

Do these strategies work? Absolutely! Many landlords, myself included, have been employing them with success for years. They can be learned. And once you understand their added value, all you need is the will and the effort to make them happen.

DEFINITION: CODEPENDENCY

Codependency is a relationship in which one person is engaged in habitual and unproductive behavior while the other person unwittingly supports that behavior. Codependents often become attached to their role as helpers and, in so doing, become less likely to improve the situation. By not pursuing eviction against a nonpaying tenant for many months, for example, a landlord may actually be encouraging a greater degree of nonpaying behavior. The tenancy relationship has become codependent. Codependent landlords may cause their tenants to become more dependent on them while codependent tenants cause their landlords to protect them, hence limiting the tenant's ability to become independent and self-reliant in the future.

Questions for reflection: When helping your tenant hurts you: The helping trap

---

1. Is the example of the landlord helping trap at all familiar? Why might it be easy to fall into this helping trap? Can you imagine that situation happening to you as a landlord? Has it ever happened to you? Please describe.

   _____

   _____

   _____

   _____

   _____

   _____

   _____

2. What do we mean by "codependency"?

   _____

   _____

   _____

   _____

   _____

   _____

   _____

3. How can you distinguish between helping that inspires a positive tenant response and helping that furthers dependency?

   _____

   _____

   _____

   _____

   _____

   _____

   _____

The Good Landlord

PART two

How to make a profit while making a difference: The Good Landlord approach

The promise and the perils

So far, I have introduced the promise and perils of making a profit while making a difference based on my own experiences and my work with many landlords over twenty-five years. I have presented three cases studies of landlords who, in different ways, are succeeding. I then presented the challenge landlords face of being stereotyped in America. The historical context of being a landlord was then discussed, tracing the rise of the tenant rights movement starting after World War II. I then laid out five common mistakes landlords make and how to avoid them.

The issue of what being helpful and community-minded can be about for Americans and landlords in particular was then introduced. I discussed the historical roots of Americans being helpful and how this has changed over time. I then presented the helping trap, a difficult dilemma that landlords face when trying to be helpful.

The Good Landlord approach

I now turn to how to succeed at making a profit while making a difference, using the Good Landlord approach. Part II starts with the idea of enlightened self-interest—what it means, how it differs from pure self-interest, and how to pursue it. I then introduce the idea that successful negotiation begins by separating people issues—namely perceptions, assumptions and emotions—from the problem to be resolved.

The three chapters that follow lay out how to put the Good Landlord approach into practice. First, I introduce four essentials for how to make landlord-tenant relationships work, namely:

- ❐ Prepare effectively and make contact
- ❐ Be friendly, but don't be their friend
- ❐ Seek to understand before being understood
- ❐ Cultivate trust with your tenant, and be reliable

I then discuss some time-tested practices for how to negotiate effectively when problems arise. The last of these three chapters introduces the Good Landlord approach to eviction, used by many landlords to prevent further losses when tenants have violated their tenancies. This approach includes what I call the Two-Track response, an approach to maintaining effective negotiations as your dispute escalates into court.

In conclusion, I discuss the question of how to put this all together—what landlords can do to turn tenants toward these practices, and what landlords can do, themselves, to rely more on these modes of action.

7

When helping your tenant helps you:
Enlightened self-interest

So far in this book, you have heard a number of stories about landlords trying to make a profit while making a difference. Although many landlords demonstrate how this is possible, by now it should be quite clear that this is not always easy. Whereas some landlords emphasize maximizing income using all reasonable means necessary, others emphasize being responsive to tenants, even if more spending is required. Landlords can thus swing between emphasizing their own needs and emphasizing the needs of their tenants. Let's name these two swings as two ends of the spectrum of whom should be served first—you or your tenants.

1. ***Serve yourself and your family first.*** Take care of yourself and your interests first, before those of other people. This view states that you should serve yourself first before serving others. Whatever needs are faced by the less fortunate, your tenants or other people, you need to care for yourself and your family first. Everyone else comes second.

2. ***Serve others first.*** Forgo your own interests so that those in greater need can be served. This view states that all of us, landlords included, should sacrifice for the sake of the needy, in order to live a responsible life. In the Biblical spirit of "loving your neighbor as yourself," landlords should defer to others, as they are able, before helping themselves.

One of the fundamental pillars of my landlording practice has been the understanding that, although my tenants and I share many interests, it is in MY interest to respond as well as I can to their interests in order for me to be able to make a profit. Let's discuss further this question of whether to serve yourself first, others first, or both.

Redefining self-interest

There is a third way between the views that one should serve oneself first versus serving others. Consider your own personal interests. They probably include:

- ❐ Being a good partner and parent
- ❐ Providing for your family
- ❐ Caring for your friends
- ❐ Enjoying your leisure time
- ❐ Staying healthy

And you, as a landlord, have other interests, such as:

- ❑ Making a profit
- ❑ Providing quality housing
- ❑ Keeping your rents affordable
- ❑ Improving the neighborhood where your property is located
- ❑ Responding to your tenants' reasonable concerns

Consider this: it's not possible to define one's own interests completely separate from the interests of others. Stated differently, it's not possible to meet one's self-interests as a landlord without incorporating the interests of your tenants, your neighbors, family members, heirs, etc.

Refer to Landlord and tenant interests, page 167

Suppose you spend your money and time improving the exterior of your building. Are you motivated solely by the wish to raise the value of your property? Or does it also give you pleasure to enhance the beauty of your building for your neighbors and the community? It doesn't have to be one or the other. Both motivations can ultimately be in your self-interest.

Enlightened self-interest

Instead of thinking about what you do as serving either yourself or others, why not consider that you can serve both? Let's formally introduce this concept of enlightened self-interest. The chart on the following page presents the differences between serving oneself, serving others, and serving both (enlightened self-interest).

Whose needs to meet first

Self	*Others*	*Enlightened self-interest*
I must look out for myself and my family, responding first and foremost to my own and my family's needs.	I need to meet my tenant's needs first before responding to my own.	I want this business to succeed for me, and also for my tenants.

When the rent is due

Self	*Others*	*Enlightened self-interest*
I need to pursue this nonpayment eviction case immediately to minimize rent losses and protect my business.	I can be flexible about the time my tenant needs to pay the back rent. I can be patient, assuming I'll be paid back in full over time.	I need to find a repayment plan that is reliable, predictable, and timely, and which has clear, enforceable consequences if not followed.

Maintenance and repair

Self	*Others*	*Enlightened self-interest*
I need to spend the least possible time and money on maintenance and repair in order to maximize profit.	I need to make sure this building is free of any defects, potential or actual, whatever the cost. There should be no need for any tenant concern. In this manner, the tenants, reciprocally, will best meet their obligations.	I need to make sure this building functions adequately for my tenants without spending excessively.

The Good Landlord

When Willie, a Cambridge-based property manager, decided in 1990 to spend $6,000 he was not required to spend to install **carbon monoxide detectors** in all 200 units he managed, he was meeting his enlightened self-interests and demonstrating super-good behaviors as well. Reducing potential carbon monoxide exposure seemed well worth the financial investment.

Jim's choice – the same Jim we met in Chapter 2 – to install a water sprinkler system in his 100-unit building is another example of enlightened self-interest with a super-good twist. Even though the law didn't require it, these investments allowed both Willie and Jim to improve tenants' health and safety, and to cut insurance costs. These landlords also slept better, knowing their tenants were better protected from possible harm.

The countless examples I have seen of landlords successfully working with tenants seeking to pay their back rent also demonstrate the power of enlightened self-interest. These landlords understand how eviction can cost many thousands in lost rent, professional fees, turnover costs, and valuable time spent. They also understand the mutually beneficial value of reaching a resolution that works for all involved.

■ *LEGAL INFO: CARBON MONOXIDE DETECTORS*

Note that most states now require **carbon monoxide detectors**. Massachusetts law and regulations now require carbon monoxide detectors to be installed in residences. (See M.G.L. chapter 148 section 26F1/2 and 527 Code of Massachusetts Regulations 31.)

Self-interest vs. enlightened self-interest: Making the distinction

The idea of enlightened self-interest need not replace traditional perspectives on self-interest. In fact, enlightened self-interest is based on the traditional idea of self-interest, but goes further. By meeting a tenant's interests, a landlord can meet her own as well. The chart on the next page shows how enlightened self-interest can include the narrower definition but go further.

READING REFERENCE: *REDISCOVERING AMERICA'S VALUES*

Throughout *Rediscovering America's Values*, Lappé discusses enlightened self-interest.

The Good Landlord

Is the market a fair way to set rents?

Self-interest	Enlightened self-interest
The only rent that is fair is the market rent.	Various criteria go into fairness: the market, as well as what rent level can maximize tenant cooperation, ease access, and ease property management challenges.

Who decides what is fair?

Self-interest	Enlightened self-interest
Don't tell me what I should do as a landlord. I own this building and can do what I want with it.	Being a landlord and a tenant entail responsibilities to each other, to the common good, and to following the law.

What role for government?

Self-interest	Enlightened self-interest
Get government out of housing.	While government does and should provide legal and regulatory oversight, landlords and tenants themselves can also accomplish a great deal privately in the name of fairness when both are principled, respectful, law-abiding, and skillful.

Is a common good possible?

Self-interest	Enlightened self-interest
No. In a pluralistic society, there are many competing interests. The notion of a "common good" is dangerous if used by those seeking to impose their will on others.	Yes, the common good can evolve from public dialogue and decision making, leading to new public norms, laws, and regulations. The common good does not require that we forego self-interest. Rather, it invites us to see our own interests as linked to others. One can pursue one's own interests as well as the common good.

The landlord opportunities map

Finding ways to meet the interests of others should not mean you cannot meet your own as well. The Landlord Opportunities Map presented below shows the five aspects of landlording which I suggest landlords focus on.

❏ Well-Maintained Building
❏ Prompt, Reliable Service
❏ Good Tenant Relations
❏ Cost Control

❏ Safe and Secure Building
❏ Habitable Apartment
❏ Quiet Enjoyment
❏ Affordable Rent

❏ Equity
❏ Liquidity
❏ Estate Planning

❏ Control Over Decisions and Time
❏ Earned Income Over Expenses
❏ Responsible Rent Setting
❏ Property Resale Value
❏ Property as Investment Vehicle
❏ Tax Advantages

❏ Attractive Building and Grounds
❏ Involvement With Community
❏ Affordable Rents
❏ Charitable Giving
❏ Volunteering

Although different landlords will tend to emphasize different aspects of the map, the vital indicator of success is whether or not landlords adequately address each. I believe—and ask you to consider—that landlords, to succeed, must ensure that *all five areas receive a minimum level of attention.*

Questions for reflection: When helping your tenant helps you: Enlightened self-interest

---

1. *What is meant by enlightened self-interest?*

_____
_____
_____
_____
_____
_____

2. *How might the pursuit of your enlightened self-interests differ from pursuing your self-interests as a small property owner? How might meeting your tenant's interests be in your OWN interests?*

_____
_____
_____
_____
_____
_____

3. *Name a specific example of when you did something for your tenants that cost you in the short term (in time, money, stress), but in actuality helped you meet your own interests.*

_____
_____
_____
_____
_____
_____

A Guide to Making a Profit While Making a Difference

8 Your tenant is not the problem:

Understanding the power of relationship

I was all ready to tell my tenant there would be a rent increase. I had made peace with the idea. I had practiced my speech. And then she called and invited me down to watch the Super Bowl. I was paralyzed!

—Cambridge, Massachusetts landlord

People vs. problems

The human complexities of being a landlord can always be a surprise, even for the most seasoned among us. What starts out as a simple communication about rent can suddenly become a perplexing problem in human relationships. Before you entered the field, you may have wondered if you could rise to the challenge of dealing with the endless repairs of plumbing and heating systems. By now, you're well aware, the real challenge and the real mystery is the people. The most important maintenance you'll ever do is not on the boiler, not on the gutters or the roof, but on the tenant relationship.

In this chapter, we will identify some major elements that contribute to healthy landlord-tenant relationships. Our goal is to keep your business and your life running smoothly, and keep you out of court. This chapter lays out the kinds of people issues you will face and an approach to unpacking them. Chapters 9, 10 and 11 will then describe how to apply these lessons in the real world.

Perceptions, assumptions, and emotions

The Super Bowl story above illustrates the landlord's classic dilemma: to raise the rent and jeopardize your good relationship with the tenant, or to hold the rent steady and jeopardize the health of your business. Two kinds of issues create tension here: substantive issues such as income, and relationship issues such as trust and predictability. Fisher and Brown characterize these differences as follows:

> *"Relationship issues concern the way we deal with people: clearly or ambiguously, honestly or deceptively, logically or emotionally, and so forth. Substantive issues are those that might typically be included in an agreement—such matters as money, dates, time, repair plans, terms, and conditions. It seems best to work on the process of a relationship—how we deal with each other—independent of all substantive differences. Try to deal with both sets of issues—people problems and substantive problems—but do not link them."*

Perceptions

Where you stand depends on where you sit.

—*Miles' Law, Rufus E. Miles, Jr.*

SOURCE

Roger Fisher and Scott Brown, *Getting Together: Building Relationships As We Negotiate* (New York: Viking-Penguin, 1989), xiv.

The landlord-tenant relationship is a drama acted out on a stage that is owned by one party and occupied primarily by the other. Complexity and vulnerability are built into this relationship from the start.

But several additional factors can further undermine this relationship if they are not watched carefully. The first factor is the difference in perception that occurs routinely, even between people who seem to be like-minded. Each party's perceptions of risks and possibilities in a situation are shaped by his or her life experiences. Where you stand does depend on where you sit.

Here's the key: each of us tends to see things in ways that favor our own interests and viewpoints. As landlords, our struggle to finance improvements looms larger than our tenant's struggle to pay the rent. Our need to reschedule a busy day to meet the plumber feels more important than the tenant's daycare schedule. In short, we each "read" our experiences in highly personal ways. As Fisher and Brown remind us, each of us:

- Sees the same events differently
- Focuses attention on different aspects of these events
- Filters and labels information to make it easy to store
- Creates a "remembered story" from the information
- Reinterprets new information to fit old views

Partisan perceptions

In the language of dispute resolution, the viewpoints that result from these different perspectives are called "partisan perceptions." This doesn't mean that they are dictated only by narrow self-interest. It simply means that experience shapes understanding, and no two people can have identical experiences.

The Good Landlord

Here are some examples of how the partisan perceptions of a landlord can differ from those of a tenant:

Quality of unit

Tenant	Landlord
I deserve a lot better quality and service!	You don't appreciate what a good unit this is for the price! Just look at its colonial charm!

Rent level

Tenant	Landlord
This place isn't worth what I'm paying!	This is a great deal! Just look at the market!

Access

Tenant	Landlord
It's always a crisis when he needs access! I always feel inconvenienced!	Tenants always let repair issues go until they turn into a crisis! Then I need access immediately, but it can take days to get in, and then I'm to blame for it!

Timing of rent payments

Tenant	Landlord
Look, you're getting the rent every month. Is it really a problem for you if it's not exactly on the first?	I have to beg and threaten just to get my rent every month! It's your responsibility!

Noise levels

Tenant	Landlord
I'm struggling to maintain order in this house! I've got three kids, two cats, and a husband who is difficult, to say the least.	When I rent an apartment, I expect my tenants to find a way to control their behavior to make life livable for the other tenants in the building.

Different stories: Why we each see the world differently

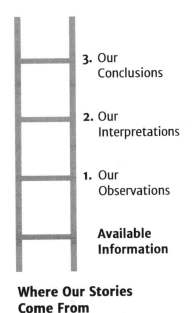

"As we move away from arguing and toward trying to understand the other person's story, it helps us to know why people have different stories in the first place. Our stories don't come out of nowhere. They aren't random. Our stories are built in often unconscious but systematic ways. First, we take in information. We experience the world—sights, sounds, and feelings. Second, we interpret what we see, hear, and feel; we give it all meaning. Then we draw conclusions about what's happening. And at each step, there is an opportunity for different people's stories to diverge.

Put simply, we all have different stories about the world because we each take in different information and then interpret this information in our own unique ways.

In difficult conversations, too often we trade only conclusions back and forth, without stepping down to where most of the real action is: the information and interpretations that lead each of us to see the world as we do."

3. Our Conclusions

2. Our Interpretations

1. Our Observations

Available Information

Where Our Stories Come From

Source: Douglas Stone, Bruce Patton, and Sheila Heen, *Difficult Conversations: How to Discuss What Matters Most* (New York: Penguin, 1999), 14.

Assumptions

Assumptions are helpful and essential for us to get by in the world. Unfortunately they often aren't accurate. These unquestioned beliefs shape what we see, think, and feel. Those that remain unconscious, however, are especially problematic. For example,

❒ We may think that shared values are necessary for a good relationship so relationships become threatened when other people's values differ from our own.

- ❐ We naturally seek a peaceful relationship, and may define peace only as avoiding disagreement. We may forget that there is another kind of peace that takes place when people acknowledge their differences in a climate of respect.
- ❐ We assume that once battle lines are drawn, people become inflexible. We may unconsciously rule out the possibility of changing the discussion so that a conflict becomes a shared problem that can be jointly solved.

And when we are at ground level observing our tenant's behavior, for example, we can make more basic assumptions such as:

- ❐ He drives a Lexus so he must have some money, but he's still not paying the rent!
- ❐ Her kids are always watching TV so she must not be a very good mom.
- ❐ The kitchen was a big mess when I went in to do a repair. She just doesn't take care of my place.

Why is it risky to make assumptions? Suppose I've been getting unusually angry at my tenant whenever he's a few days late paying the rent. Upon reflection, I realize that he reminds me of a very difficult tenant who began withholding rent and whom I eventually evicted after a prolonged dispute. My anger now is a sign of the powerlessness I felt in that previous situation. Once I gain the perspective that the past is fueling the intensity of my current feelings, and that the situations are not the same, I can become calmer. I may still take action to encourage this tenant to pay on time, but I won't be reacting emotionally, and assuming the current situation will automatically play out as the last one did. I will thus be acting more effectively.

Emotions

Finally, emotion is a major human factor attached to dealings with tenants. The fact that emotions are irrational or, more accurately, non-rational, does not mean they are unimportant. Emotions are important signals about your response to your environment.

Not surprisingly, our strongest emotions—anger, frustration or fear, for example—are often the hardest to manage, and at the root of destructive behavior when differences arise. Making peace with your emotions is the antidote to being overcome by them. When landlords are managing their emotions effectively, they can harness them to help resolve disputes.

Learning to manage your emotions so they don't manage you can greatly enhance your success. The practice of mindfulness offers one way to do this. **Mindfulness** can help you avoid becoming

See page 128 and Appendix C

Two ways landlords can manage emotions:

Cathy

When Cathy, a landlord I know, let it loose one day with her tenant Alice over an access issue, she expressed a great deal of emotion—but her tenant still didn't know what she was feeling. "I mean... I can't believe you would even... Why would you ever??!!... What were you thinking?!?!? How could you have?!?!?..." Cathy blurted to Alice. "Her jumbled, unfinished sentences kept spilling out loudly without any control or direction," Alice told me, "but I couldn't tell if she was feeling angry, anxious, or sad, let alone what she wanted." Cathy, unfortunately, was expressing a great deal of emotion without effectively conveying her feelings, let alone her wants and needs.

Rinaldo

Rinaldo, another landlord I know, expresses his emotions judiciously and effectively when he talks. He carefully chooses his words and tone of voice and conveys his emotions quite persuasively. "I will respond to this repair issue tomorrow," Rinaldo said respectfully but firmly, "and want to make an access plan that is flexible for me while respecting your privacy." In this case, although Rinaldo was quite upset after many days of trying to arrange access, he channeled his palpable anger into problem solving rather than yelling and screaming. His tenants were moved because he did not lose control.

derailed by difficult emotions, during negotiations or whenever they overwhelm your reasoning and thinking.

Unconditionally constructive behavior

All of these human factors add to the tension and complexity of a conflict, all the more so because they can seem so intangible. When these factors are understood, conflicts do not go away but they do become more manageable. This is because people and social groups have legitimate conflicts of interest due to their different positions and viewpoints.

The subject of rent is one of the clearest examples of genuine tension, if not outright conflict, between people with potentially conflicting interests. In purely economic terms, whereas the tenant has an interest in paying the lowest possible rent, the landlord has an interest in receiving the highest possible rent. The landlord has to consider perceptions, assumptions, and emotions when managing tenant relationships, whereas rent collection is substantive and concrete. No amount of careful communication or insight into the tenant relationship can alter this basic fact.

DEFINITION: *MINDFULNESS*

Mindfulness refers to being completely in touch with and aware of the present moment, as well as taking a non-evaluative and non-judgmental approach to your inner experience. For example, a mindful approach to one's inner experience is simply viewing "thoughts as thoughts" as opposed to evaluating certain thoughts as positive or negative. See Appendix C.

The term comes from Eastern spiritual and religious traditions such as Zen Buddhism. Mental health professionals are beginning to recognize that mindfulness can have many benefits for people suffering from anxiety, depression, and other difficulties.

SOURCE: *UNCONDITIONALLY CONSTRUCTIVE BEHAVIOR*

The application of **unconditionally constructive behavior** has been extensively explored in Fisher and Brown, *Getting Together*.

When landlords are *soft on the person* (factoring in perceptions, emotions, and assumptions), but *hard on the problem* (focusing like a laser beam on getting the rent), they lay the groundwork for establishing what can be called an unconditionally constructive approach. By unconditionally constructive, I mean acting in a constructive manner regardless of how your tenant acts.

When you employ unconditionally constructive practices, you adopt guidelines that will be good for the relationship and good for you, whether or not your tenant follows the same guidelines. In other words, you strive to treat your tenants respectfully whether or not they show respect for you. This

Refer to Landlord and tenant interests, page 167

assumes a common interest—which is usually present in a landlord-tenant relationship. Both landlord and tenant need what each provides: timely rent payment, responsible property maintenance, and the other services and amenities built into rental housing. Unconditionally constructive practices can be enhanced by this interdependence.

In other words, you can invest in tenant relationships, which can pay many dividends, while being hard on the problem, which can include:

- ❏ Getting the rent on time
- ❏ Securing reasonable rent increases
- ❏ Accessing the unit reliably

If you want to succeed, many experienced landlords remind me, you have to be hard on the problem. Being soft on the person however—building effective relationships with your tenants, whether or not they are difficult—can make this possible. Being soft on the person can create the climate needed for negotiating effectively while preparing to litigate if necessary. It will help you stay in control.

Questions for reflection: Your tenant is not the problem: Understanding the power of relationship

---

1. Have you ever had an experience with a tenant in which you made an assumption but soon discovered that you had jumped to a conclusion too quickly? What was the assumption you made? Describe the experience.

   _____

   _____

   _____

2. What is it about dealing with difficult tenant situations that can make you angry?

   _____

   _____

   _____

3. How can you best handle anger when addressing tenant issues?

   _____

   _____

   _____

4. How have strong emotions affected your thinking, if at all? What do you do when strong emotions are making it hard to decide your best plan of action?

   _____

   _____

   _____

5. As you think about your relationship with your tenants, do you notice any patterns? Are your relationships too often adversarial, or too often conciliatory?

   _____

   _____

   _____

9 Making tenant relationships work: Four essentials

People who produce good results feel good about themselves.

—Ken Blanchard
Putting the One Minute Manager to Work

It is no secret that most landlords own rental property to make a profit. And, in spite of a number of inherent risks and challenges built into the business, most do make a profit.

For tenants, however, the reality of needing to pay rent can inject considerable tension into the landlord-tenant relationship. When tenants think their hard-earned dollars are dedicated to making a profit for their landlord, they naturally get angry and resentful. While a tenant is earning eight, twelve, or fifteen dollars an hour at best, they assume, the landlord is "sitting on his duff," perking up just in time for collection day. Because most tenants believe their landlords are doing quite well, and with little effort, landlord concessions such as forgiving some back rent seem fair and equitable. Landlords should make concessions, tenants argue, to balance the scales.

If you assume that your tenants think this way, you may be less reactive to them, particularly when they become defensive or wholly self-serving. But how can you maximize cooperation with your tenant when all he sees is that you're in the privileged position? Here are four essentials—call them habits or principles—for building an effective relationship and maximizing tenant cooperation in any situation.

1. Prepare effectively—and make contact
2. Be friendly—but don't be their friend
3. Seek to understand before being understood
4. Be reliable—and cultivate trust

1. Prepare effectively— and make contact

It's already the 19th of the month and Angela, your tenant, still owes you rent. You've already called her three times but she hasn't returned your calls. You can imagine why: Angela would first have to explain why she has not called before even acknowledging she owes the rent. Who wants to admit they are guilty? Committing to a payment plan is hard enough. But acknowledging one's negligence can feel overwhelming to a tenant. Most would rather avoid being confronted by an impatient landlord—even if the consequences are worse later. Why face the pain now?

You may understand Angela's story, but what about you? Not only are you owed the rent, but you have to do the pursuing. Time is on Angela's side, not yours. Every day you don't take action, you lose more rent. But approaching your tenant is quite difficult because, by now, you are angry at her. Approaching her when angry could backfire. The tenant could take the "moral high ground" and make this about your anger rather than about the rent. But repressing your anger is no solution either. It will only make you feel more resentful.

This kind of case presents a profound problem for today's landlords. However clear your goals, situations like this can turn you into an emotional wreck! Being a landlord presents an extraordinary opportunity, however, to develop new skills for managing stress. Dealing with stressful situations effectively will increase your confidence and your ability to solve problems! Your catch-phrase can become; "It may be stressful out there, but it need not be stressful in here."

When you prepare effectively using the Good Landlord approach, you can:

▲ *Become more calm and less stressed*

▲ *Attain the information, attitude, and new skills needed to respond effectively*

▲ *Prevent disputes from escalating*

▲ *Resolve disputes more effectively*

Preparing effectively includes the following steps:

▲ *Take stock*

▲ *Assess how ready you are*

▲ *Listen to yourself first*

Once you've prepared effectively, making contact will give you the chance to resolve problems with your tenant before things escalate. You'll spend the least amount of time and money while getting the best results.

Take stock

What approach will allow you to resolve issues successfully with your tenants? The suggestions that follow should not be applied as a formula. Consider tempering them with your own wisdom, intuition, and experience.

Taking stock means first stepping back from the situation you're facing. This can allow you to make a plan for moving forward, including your negotiating strategy and the terms of an agreement you might accept. You can then envision alternative ways to satisfy your interests.

The Good Landlord

Refer to Dispute Resolution Prep Sheet, page 235.

You need to take stock of:

▲ *The legal issues involved*
▲ *The interpersonal issues involved*
▲ *Your personal readiness for making contact*
▲ *Your interests*
▲ *The results you are seeking*

In addition, there are underlying aspects to take stock of which include:

❐ Your own assumptions, perceptions, and emotions
❐ Your tenants' assumptions, perceptions, and emotions
❐ Each party's style of handling conflict

Taking stock of all these factors can stir up plenty of emotion. And stirred up is just what you *don't want* when preparing to negotiate. When you are convinced you know as much as possible about the situation at hand, stop and review what you have learned. Some of the charged emotions in disputes, like blame or anger, result from the understandable desire to change the other party or exact revenge. Personal peace and strategic advantage, however, come from understanding the underlying causes of the tenant's behavior (whether or not you approve of them) and accepting people as they are. Making peace with this situation will allow you to make choices based on what is effective, not on what is making you angry and resentful.

FINDING SOLUTIONS: MAKE PEACE WITH YOURSELF

In addition to bringing an understanding of your tenant's situation to your own peacemaking process, there are other things you can do as well. Try taking a short walk before further words are uttered. Consider taking five or more long, slow, deep breaths. Anything you can do that will bring a sense of inner calm to an emotionally-charged situation will increase your success with your tenant.

Assess how ready you are

This is the next step in preparing to respond. As you move forward to resolve the nonpayment issue (or any other issues), you first need to assess your readiness. What is your state of mind? What *zone* are you in?

In any interpersonal contact, we can find ourselves in one of three zones:

Understandably enough, many of us like to stay in our comfort zone. "Comfort" sounds and feels good. Most of us prefer this zone as a way of avoiding confrontation. This avoidance explains why many landlords let their attorneys do the talking.

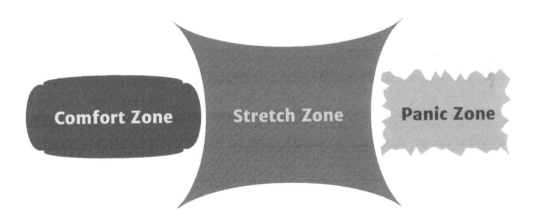

With respect to the current conflict, consider the meaning of each of these zones for you. What takes you to the edge of your comfort zone? Meeting your tenant? Speaking with your tenant's attorney? Just thinking about how to respond? It may not take much to move into the stretch zone.

Maybe you're one of the fortunate landlords who can get through the discussions, the questions, and the planning without undue anxiety. Maybe you begin to move into the stretch zone only when you are asked to consider certain unpleasant options, such as surrendering control or taking a large financial hit.

For many people, however, feeling stretched almost immediately moves them into the panic zone. For them, too much uncertainty is just too stressful. Does this describe you? If so, you have a choice: you can stay that way and opt for self-protection, or you can extend your boundaries ever-so-gently, and become comfortable in a new stretch zone. Part of the trick in developing this comfort is making smart choices that help keep a situation from escalating out of control.

Listen to yourself first

The next step in preparing effectively is to *listen to yourself first*. Becoming aware of what is happening inside you can help you gauge how well you will communicate. Failure to look within can lead you to behave in ways that are counterproductive.

For instance, if your anger is overwhelming you as you begin a conversation with a tenant, you may express the anger in ways that distract you from what you really need, namely the rent! If you express too much anger, you might damage your goodwill with the tenant at the time you most need a good working relationship.

By contrast, when you listen to yourself first, becoming aware of your thoughts and emotions, you will be better able to manage and express yourself as you pursue the rent. Listening to yourself first will also allow you to hear your tenant better. You will still be able to speak up while making it easier to resolve the issue of back rent. You also will have affirmed your common humanity, which is always a good place to start.

Instead of a yelling match, a conversation could go like this:

> **Landlord:** I'm calling because I haven't received the rent. You usually are on time and you call me back, so I assume something's up. Is everything okay?"
>
> **Tenant:** I've been having a terrible time. My job has been reduced to part-time and my mother is sick.
>
> **Landlord:** I'm sorry to hear that. I can imagine how hard these situations are. How are you holding up?
>
> **Tenant:** Well, it's been rough. I haven't been as on top of things as I usually am. Things have been difficult given my mom's treatments and my job. I'm sorry I haven't been in touch and I know that I owe you money.
>
> **Landlord:** I'm sorry that you're going through all that. And it has been unusual to not hear from you. I understand that calling me back can be tough to do when things have been hard. Let's make that easier to do in the future. I have some suggestions, which include needing to resolve the immediate issue of rent.
>
> **Tenant:** I know. I just haven't been able to bring myself to deal with it. I think I can now, though. Here's what I can pay you by next week...

Notice that by first listening to and expressing concern for your tenant, you will establish an atmosphere in which your own needs, as well as the tenant's, can be addressed. Later on in the conversation, you can express your need, in the future, to hear from her as soon as a problem emerges. When you use your diplomacy skills to make such a demand, you will be more successful, and see more money in your pocket.

Make contact

Problem solving doesn't happen in the abstract. Neither does it happen when you're pacing the kitchen floor pondering the principles of dispute resolution. It happens when you and your tenant make contact. Your willingness to initiate this contact is the first step.

The Good Landlord

Consider your approach

▲ *If you are one who likes to make contact and your tenant is an avoider, you will want to approach your tenant in a way that's gentle enough not to be overwhelming, but still firm.*

▲ *If you are an avoider, you might remember the advice of psychologist Susan Jeffers to "feel the fear and do it anyway."*

▲ *If you're an accommodator and your tenant is a problem solver or fighter, you will want to show enough assertiveness that you will be taken seriously, while also projecting good cheer and confidence that successful problem solving is possible.*

Consider how to make contact

▲ *Do you prefer catching a tenant in the driveway, calling her cell phone, sending an e-mail, texting, or leaving a note at her door?*

▲ *Who is the best person to communicate with for each apartment? Is it the tenant himself, his girlfriend, or someone else?*

▲ *Which style of communication suits you best? Do you prefer to take orders and give orders, or do you prefer to work things out through listening and problem solving?*

Pay attention to timing

We often think we have to resolve every issue immediately. This is a set-up for failure. Finding the right time to talk may be as important as the message itself. Consider your tenant's schedule, and your own, so that you can make contact when you each have enough time to speak calmly with each other.

The first conversation you have on the issues should be the beginning, not the end, of your negotiations. The best scenario is to open up communication slowly, briefly stating your concerns and hearing a short version of the tenant's. Then, try to do the following:

- ❐ Establish (and preferably agree upon) the agenda. Decide what needs to be discussed.
- ❐ Establish a timeframe. Decide by when you would like to see the issues resolved. Do you and the tenant need to resolve your issues today, by next week, over the next three months, or when?
- ❐ Determine what information you both know now. Then, determine what information you both need to move forward.

How you make contact and address timing issues can make a big difference. Timing matters.

2. Be friendly—but don't be their friend

Conventional wisdom holds that the working relationship between landlords and tenants should be as impersonal as possible. "Don't try to be friends with your tenants," says one school of thought. However, if this rules out any chance for meaningful communication, you will lose a valuable tool for making your tenant relationships work.

Consider, instead, that a healthy and productive landlord-tenant relationship could be friendly (while it may or may not grow close). It is humanized by small acts of neighborliness and mutual support, from Super Bowl invitations to sharing a garden, which can lead to better communication when problems arise. These efforts can work if each party maintains healthy boundaries, makes clear agreements, and follows through reliably. In addition, each party has to make his or her needs known.

The Good Landlord

Being friendly with tenants does not mean you need to always give in or be overly flexible. Landlords should be hard on the problem, namely to get their needs met. In my experience, it is entirely possible to do this while maintaining a friendly rapport with tenants. And when you consider that one of your interests is in resolving disputes as peacefully as possible, a friendly rapport can be invaluable!

Carlos, a landlord I've worked with, practices this skill quite effectively, making sure to maintain a close connection with his tenants. "I recently attended my tenant Dalia's kid's graduation party," Carlos told me. Carlos is in and out of Dalia's house regularly, catching a meal, or lingering after a repair job. Carlos communicates thoroughly, makes timely repairs, and often brings a snack when invited. So when Carlos's eviction case suddenly appeared one day in court where I mediate, I followed up. "I've been pushing to get the rent this month," he told me. "I'm moving forward in court if we can't work something out. And believe me I'm trying!" Carlos understands how to be soft on the person but hard on the problem.

How can you be friendly with your tenant without becoming their friend? Two helpful practices will be introduced below. The first—expressing appreciation—can make a big difference.

Express appreciation

Everyone wants to be appreciated. Being appreciated raises our self-esteem. It opens us up to listening. It increases our cooperation. To strengthen relationships, therefore, one low-cost, low-risk step you can take is to express appreciation, not only for your tenants, but for anyone

---

SOURCE: *EXPRESS APPRECIATION*

The ideas behind **expressing appreciation** are introduced and greatly expanded on in Stone, Patton, and Heen, *Difficult Conversations*.

else who works with you as a landlord (such as your contractors, attorney, neighbors, etc.).

But why should you express appreciation for someone who, in your view, may not deserve it? *To express appreciation doesn't mean you have to concede power, withdraw rights, or make concessions.* One can appreciate another's point of view without agreeing with it. There may be much about your tenant's behavior that you don't appreciate. You may think that some tenants deserve to be evicted and punished for what they have done. Although it may be a challenge to withhold the epithets and threats in these cases, it is often in your interest to do so. Choosing to convey what you do appreciate will likely play to your favor. You can make a practice of expressing only what is helpful or constructive.

Building successful relationships depends on nothing less than how one cultivates understanding and mutual respect. One way to do this is to express appreciation. Here are three tips for how to do this.

1. **Decide the best format for conveying your appreciation.** Here are a few options to consider:

   Write a formal letter. This can demonstrate your commitment to conveying your message.

   Call. "I just called to thank you for coordinating the carpet cleaning service" can help remind the tenant that you appreciate what he has done.

   Communicate in person, on-the-spot. This is the easy one that we all forget. If you can make it a habit to express appreciation in the moment, you'll often get a thank you, and more cooperation in return.

   E-mail or text. This can accomplish your communication goals in a simple way but can sometimes be impersonal, so be careful.

2. **Be specific.** Acknowledge the specific behavior your tenant exhibited, when they did it and why it was important. For example: "Last night you called me twice to make sure I knew about the unusual sounds in the basement. This helped me do a timely repair that avoided a major breakdown of the third floor heating system. That made a big difference for me! Thank you!"

3. ***Make it genuine.*** Finding a way to show your tenant that you do care can make a big difference in securing the cooperation you want. Just like your kids, your partner, your boss, your coworkers, your friends, your neighbors, and everyone else in your life, your tenant can tell if you're being authentic or not. Being genuine, even in moments when you may not be feeling warmly toward the tenant, can help your cause. Here are some tips.

❐ Use a positive tone
❐ Look your tenant in the eye
❐ Speak from your heart
❐ Listen to your tenant after you make your point

You will also strengthen your relationship when you express the value of what your tenant is thinking, doing or feeling.

Consider expressing the value in what your tenant:

Thinks

I appreciate that you express concern about keeping my costs down for the basement repairs I'm doing. Thank you.

Does

I appreciate that you made the effort to:

▲ *Keep your unit clean*
▲ *Clean the hallways*
▲ *Clean up around the trash area*
▲ *Express your appreciation after seeing the repairs I have made.*

Feels

I admire the pride you put into your efforts to:

▲ *Maintain peace and quiet on the premises*
▲ *Alert tenants in the building regarding possible vandalism*

Make deposits into the Tenant Relationship Bank

What if you could deposit some money in the bank from situations when you acted most helpfully and compassionately toward your tenant? You could then withdraw this money to buy cooperation and flexibility when your tenancy relationship became strained. If you spent down your account too far, you would risk reduced cooperation and flexibility.

Your tenant relationship can be actively promoted in this way. Stephen Covey calls this "deposits into" and "withdrawals from" the bank. Let's imagine that landlords can make deposits into and withdrawals from the Tenant Relationship Bank. These might include:

- ❑ **Favors unrelated to landlord or tenant roles,** for instance when a landlord drives a tenant to a job interview or a tenant gives the landlord produce from her garden
- ❑ **Initiatives above and beyond the tenancy contract,** for example when a landlord installs energy-saving lighting equipment or a tenant offers to do small repairs
- ❑ **Flexibility**, such as allowing a normally reliable tenant to pay rent in installments during a difficult time

Over time, these investments in a healthy relationship will be beneficial to you as a landlord. These deposits in the tenant relationship bank represent opportunities to secure future tenant cooperation when you really need it. For instance, you may need to ask your tenant to spend a cold winter weekend without heat until your plumber can make a repair on Monday morning. You may need to enlist your tenant's help to temporarily stop a plumbing leak by turning off a water shut-off valve while you are away. Cultivating a good relationship with your tenant can incline him or her to

---

SOURCE: TENANT RELATIONSHIP BANK

Adapted from concept of the Emotional Bank Account in Stephen R. Covey, *The Seven Habits of Highly Effective People* (New York: Free Press, 1989), 188.

return favors when you really need them. This can only add to your success as a landlord. And when disputes arise, the deposits you have made will help reduce potential conflict and keep the focus on common interests.

Maximizing your deposits while minimizing withdrawals, as described above, can be of enormous help to you as a landlord.

Some possible deposits and withdrawals

Activity	Deposits	Withdrawals
Repairs	Making a needed repair before your tenant calls to request it	Putting off a needed repair for more than a week
Access	Letting a tenant—who misplaced her key —into her unit at 2 a.m.	Not calling a tenant back for 12 hours when she is locked out
Payment plans	Agreeing to a tenant plan to repay a few months' rent over time	Serving an eviction notice the day after your tenant says she needs a couple days to pay the rent
Favors	Taking your tenant's trash to the curb when the tenant is out of town	Not calling the tenant back after being asked to do a favor
Rent increases	Delaying a scheduled rent increase by two months, as requested by the tenant, to accommodate tenant's short-term drop in income	Not calling the tenant back, and opposing the request after it is made

3. Seek to understand before being understood

A landlord couple I worked with a couple of years ago had done almost everything right in their acquisition of a run-down apartment building. They devoted weekend after weekend to a cleanup campaign. They trimmed trees and shrubs. They graded the slope, landscaped the grounds, and planted tulips. Just as they were finishing, the front door to the building opened. Out came a tenant who had lived there for four years, whom they had only briefly met. He glared at them and asked mournfully, "Why did you remove my beautiful hydrangea bush?"

That relationship was born hostile, partly because this tenant was difficult to please, but also because the new landlords had not performed the simple act of checking in with these tenants before making changes in the environment. Some people like hydrangea. Some people like wood chips. Knowing something about the tastes, lifestyle, socioeconomic background, and special circumstances of your tenants from the beginning can make a big difference.

You cannot meet all your tenants' interests, but if you can show them how your needs and theirs overlap, you can create a cooperative, mutually beneficial relationship. In establishing such a healthy working relationship, no advice is more valuable than "Seek to understand before being understood."

SOURCE: *SEEK TO UNDERSTAND*

"**Seek to understand before being understood**" was popularized in Covey, *Seven Habits*, 235.

The value of listening

If you are like most, you have learned to appreciate the importance of listening, whether to your tenant or to anyone else. Given all the listening we do, though, you would think we would be good at it! When most of us talk to each other, unfortunately, we do not listen attentively. We are often distracted, half listening, half thinking about something else. We assume we have already heard what the speaker is saying many times before.

Take Sue, a landlord who called me one day, upset that her tenant, Rafael, had been parking his bicycle in the front hallway for months. Not only because this was prohibited in his lease, but because other tenants were complaining, Sue finally confronted him. Rafael was trying to tell Sue that his bicycle was his only form of transportation and there was no basement access. Sue had decided not to allow him basement access for his bicycle, however. But all she could do to communicate this was to interrupt, berate and threaten him. Rafael finally walked away angry, leaving Sue without a plan. Only after the damage was done—Rafael became quite pushy over minor repair issues and fought a minor rent increase—did Sue finally do what she could have done much earlier, namely to problem solve over where to put the bicycle. She resolved the issue by freeing up some space under the front porch.

How can you listen in a genuine manner when, like Sue, you are trying to satisfy your own needs and win arguments? If you are like most people, you probably seek *first to be understood*. Most people listen with the intent to reply, not to understand. We listen while preparing what we are going to say, filtering everything through our own life experiences. And in doing so, we may ignore the other person completely, pretending that we are listening while selectively hearing only certain parts of the conversation, often missing the meaning entirely. Does this ring true for you?

Many of us are on automatic so often that we do not realize how much we are communicating from our own perspective only. Not that our own opinions and interpretations are not helpful, but when and how we use them can make a big difference. If others perceive you as forcing your opinions and interpretations on them, they will be less likely to cooperate.

"Now wait a minute," you might reply. "I'm just trying to relate to the person by drawing on my own experiences. Is that so bad?" In some situations, self-referential responses may be appropriate, such as when another person asks for help and shows interest in your point of view, or when there is already some trust in the relationship. But in most cases, listening to your tenant before introducing your own opinions will be in your self-interest. This invaluable lesson has helped me many times.

True listening means being willing to suspend your own viewpoint and pay attention to the other person. Using this technique can help you to improve your ability to persuade and negotiate. Your ability to listen in this manner may be one of the most important skills you can cultivate.

We listen for four reasons:

▲ To obtain information
▲ To enjoy

▲ To understand
▲ To learn

Becoming a better listener

The way to become a better listener is to pay attention not only to the words that the speaker is saying but also to her tone of voice and body language. To do this well, you also need to avoid being distracted by whatever else may be going on around you. You also need to avoid preparing your counter arguments. First try to understand the substance of what your tenant is saying and the emotion behind it.

To help us appreciate the power of listening, ask yourself if you have ever been in a conversation when you wondered if the other person was actually listening to you. You may have wondered if he or she even heard your message.

In contrast, remember a conversation in which someone truly listened to you. How did this experience feel?

Five elements of effective listening

a. **Pay attention.** Give the tenant your undivided attention and acknowledge what she is saying:

- ☐ Look at the speaker directly
- ☐ Put aside distracting thoughts
- ☐ Avoid being distracted by the environment around you
- ☐ Pay attention to the speaker's body language

b. **Show that you are listening.** As a listener, your role is to acknowledge what your tenants are telling you. Acknowledgment can be something as simple as a nod of the head or a simple "yes" or "uh-huh." You are not necessarily agreeing with the person, but you are indicating that you are listening. You can also show that you are listening by:

- ☐ Smiling and expressing interest through facial expressions
- ☐ Maintaining an open posture
- ☐ Using body language that expresses interest
- ☐ Summarizing, such as saying: "What I'm hearing is..." or "Sounds like you are saying..."
- ☐ Nodding occasionally

c. **Don't interrupt.** Interrupting is a waste of time. It frustrates the speaker, reduces the chance for each to be heard, and limits full understanding. Allow your tenant to finish speaking.

d. Ask for more information. Asking for more information helps you to understand the situation better and helps your counterpart to be more understood. If you find yourself getting confused by what someone said, ask for more information: "I may not be understanding you correctly. What I thought you just said is ABC. Is that what you meant? Am I missing anything?"

e. Respond appropriately. How you respond can inspire respect and understanding with your tenant. When you respond appropriately, you are setting the stage for constructive negotiations while building trust. This is in sharp contrast to attacking your tenant or putting her down. You can:

- ☐ Express that you understand what your tenant is saying
- ☐ When appropriate, validate what the tenant may be feeling or thinking
- ☐ Find the right time to express your opinions
- ☐ Be candid and straightforward
- ☐ Use a calming tone

It can take a lot of effort and determination to be an effective listener. When you can set aside other thoughts and behaviors in order to fully concentrate on what is being said, your effectiveness will improve dramatically. Asking questions and paraphrasing to ensure you understand the message will also help significantly. Effective listening can make the difference between a tenant offering concessions to resolve a dispute vs. increasing the threats and escalating the dispute.

4: Be reliable—and cultivate trust

The value of trust

Trust is often seen as the most important element of an effective working relationship. When trust levels are high, you can accept what is said without question and rely on promises made. Trust among businesses enables thousands of deals to close every day based on a phone conversation or a handshake. Decision-making and action can flow more easily when trust is high.

When landlords and tenants trust one another, tenants can make late rent payments, and landlords can delay repairs for a couple of days, all without issue. Not that late rent payments or repair delays are encouraged, but when there's trust, flexibility is possible and problems become more solvable.

When landlords and tenants distrust each other, every little wrong becomes magnified. Landlords and tenants avoid talking things through. They rely more on threats and adversarial procedures to get things done.

Most of us know the value of building trust but do not always know how to cultivate it. We might think, for example, that the goal is to become unconditionally trusting, but this could be dangerous. To move from skepticism toward trust, we first need to build a foundation. If I want to increase your trust in me, I will need to be reliable. If I want to become more trusting of you, I will need more evidence of your reliability.

SOURCE: *CULTIVATE TRUST*

The ideas in this section are adapted from Fisher and Brown's notion of "Be wholly trustworthy, but not wholly trusting" in Fisher and Brown, *Getting Together*, 107.

Successful landlord-tenant relationships depend on increasing your own reliability, while also dealing effectively with your tenant's reliability. Both parties have to step up, in other words, for tenant relationships to work. Let's look at this more closely.

Two steps to building trust

How can you inspire people to want to trust you? As discussed earlier, listening is key. People first need to feel genuinely heard. Then, they can become open to hearing your ideas, your point of view and your counsel.

The example we set, our personal conduct, can also inspire trust. How you live your life is more important than what people say or think about you. (*However if you are getting a certain kind of negative feedback on a regular basis, take time to consider the grain of truth that may be there. Ask friends—and perhaps even tenants—for feedback. Be open to working on making some changes in your behavior.*) It is the kind of person you really are, your character, that people pick up on and that can inspire trust.

How can we inspire trust?

1. **Step back and assess your own reliability.** Much of human behavior is unpredictable, we know, because different things happen at different times. What if you tell your tenant you will need access to the unit at 9 a.m. tomorrow but, truth be told, you are not sure this will work. What if you promise to meet your tenant Tuesday at 7 p.m. to discuss the rent, but then decide to break the date, minutes beforehand, because something sufficiently important (in your own eyes) came up. Are you being unreliable? Are you communicating carelessly or treating promises lightly? If you can take a step back to assess how reliable you are, you can find out just what it takes to increase your reliability.

The Good Landlord

2. *Increase your reliability and trustworthiness by improving your own conduct.* It is in my interest to be trusted. If you trust me, life will be easier. I can ask you at the last minute, if I have to, to replace the windows on Thursday instead of Tuesday. I can call you at the last minute for access. We will be better able to resolve disputes.

What can you do to increase others' trust in you? Here are five guidelines.

---

a. **Be predictable:** *Improve your own predictability. Set up a schedule and follow it. If you cannot guarantee that the plumber will finish by 5 p.m., make sure the tenant knows the back-up plan.*

b. **Be clear:** *Use language that does not convey a commitment unless you can keep the commitment. Instead of saying: "I SHOULD be home at 10 p.m.," say: "I can't make a commitment. If all goes well, I may be home at 10, but it may be later."*

c. **Take your own promises to others seriously:** *Make fewer promises. And be scrupulous in keeping the promises you do make, even when they seem unimportant. Arrive on time at all meetings. Be reliable about the small things.*

d. **Be honest:** *Honesty doesn't require full disclosure. Greater disclosure between tenant and landlord makes it easier to solve problems, but nondisclosure is sometimes appropriate. A landlord can listen to a tenant apologize about the frequent late night disturbances, but not disclose that he has friends or other tenants "watching" this tenant.*

e. **Deal with problems BEFORE they happen:** *Tell your tenants the plumber will likely show up by 5 p.m., but in case he does not, (a) here's a shower option, and (b) the plumber will definitely be there by 9 a.m. the next day.*

Dealing with unreliable tenants

Trust, but verify.

—*Russian proverb*

Just two weeks after Amy, a tenant, had threatened Dan, a landlord I knew, with a $10,000 lawsuit, Amy was inviting Dan over for tea to see a new computer graphic program she had developed. When Dan, who I coached for a number of months, first rejected the idea, Amy asked Dan again, which confused Dan greatly. Although Amy was fighting with Dan in one moment, in the next she was pursuing a personal connection.

Amy's personal gesture allowed Dan to raise the issue of the lawsuit. She told Dan she had not intended to follow through at all with the lawsuit, but was just frustrated by their lack of communication over a recent roof repair. Dan still felt highly guarded in spite of her friendly gesture, but he learned an important lesson about trust.

Sometimes your perception that your tenant is untrustworthy may make it harder to have a working relationship. Don't throw up your hands in despair, however erratic a tenant's behavior may be. Ask yourself instead how your actions may be preventing the tenant from becoming more trustworthy. Perhaps you are behaving in ways that cause the tenant to be less reliable than he or she would otherwise be.

Let's look at a few issues involving trust, and how they might be resolved.

The Good Landlord

Do we overload trust?

Do we trust too much? We sometimes trust others when it is not appropriate to do so. For example, we might trust the tenant to be home in order to let a contractor in when the tenant could not be relied on to do this.

Act to reduce risks.

Don't rely on pure trust. *Trust, but verify.* For example:

▲ Ask a tenant for a last month's rent even if you trust she will pay the rent for the last month.

▲ Do a walkthrough of a unit even if the outgoing tenant tells you the unit is in good shape.

▲ After accepting your tenant's apology for her late night disturbances, you keep a watchful eye on this tenant and remind her that there will be consequences if the behavior continues.

Do we trust too little?

Sometimes we watch tenants too closely. It can be risky not to take risks. For example:

▲ We spend too much time training the tenant to do the pruning after they have listed their gardening credentials.

Trust them when they deserve it.

For example, as we'll learn in Stage 1 of the Two-Track approach to handling eviction issues, you can:

▲ Offer a two-week period for your tenant to pay a portion of the back rent to see if she meets her commitments.

▲ Give your tenant a chance to fix the toilet as barter, but also go over to the unit to see if she has followed through.

Do we overly praise or overly blame?	Communicate both praise and blame precisely.
We can sometimes treat a minor offense as if it were a federal crime. It should be obvious that this behavior will not gain you many friends.	Treat problematic behavior as a joint problem, not a crime. Treat every broken promise as a matter of future concern for the relationship. Look to the future, get more specific, and talk about conduct, not people.

Example: Your tenant shows up one hour late for an appointment.

Limited response:	Constructive response (using measured tone):
"Late again! No wonder nobody trusts you."	"I've been waiting for about an hour. Did something come up? This upsets me, but perhaps I was unclear regarding what time we agreed to meet. What happened? *(Pause for response and put on your listening cap.)* It would help me to plan my time better and avoid upset if we could clarify our time commitments. What would you suggest?"

The Good Landlord

Questions for reflection: Making tenant relationships work: Four essentials

---

1. *Prepare effectively—and make contact*

   a. Do you prefer to stay primarily in your comfort zone?

   _____

   _____

   b. Do you find yourself in your stretch zone as a landlord? What has this been like?

   _____

   _____

   c. Have you found yourself sometimes in your panic zone? What has that been like?

   _____

   _____

   d. How well do you think you prepare for discussing difficult, eviction-related issues with your tenant? What would you like to improve?

   _____

   _____

2. *Be friendly—But don't be their friend*

   a. How friendly do you like to be with your tenants? Do you get satisfaction from this?

   _____

   _____

   b. Are there ways in which your friendliness might compromise your ability to set proper boundaries and protect your interests as a landlord? How?

   _____

   _____

   c. What are examples in your current approach (or your new planned approach) for how to be friendly but not be their friend?

   _____

   _____

3. *Seek first to understand before being understood—and listen*

   a. Think of a time when someone didn't listen to you before telling you what you should do. How did that feel to you?

_____

_____

   b. Are there ever times when you fail to listen well to others? Spend some time wondering about that and deciding whether and how you might listen better in these situations.

_____

_____

_____

4. *Be reliable—and cultivate trust with your tenant*

   a. Is your behavior ever inconsistent? Is your conduct ever erratic? Do you ever not follow through as planned? What is it about your behavior that may make others not trust you?

_____

_____

_____

   b. Has a relationship in which you trusted the other person backfired recently? What happened? How did you feel? How did it affect future expectations?

_____

_____

_____

   c. How might a trusting relationship have helped you recently?

_____

_____

_____

10
Getting what you need:
Negotiation fundamentals

You can't always get what you want.
But if you try sometime, you just might find, you
get what you need.

—*Mick Jagger and Keith Richards*

Diplomacy is the art of allowing the
other person to get your way.

—*Daniel Varè*

Imagine two roommates, Sally and Philip, each returning home one evening expecting to eat the same orange.

Sally: Hey Philip... that's my orange! You know I set it aside earlier today.

Philip: That's not true! All our other housemates, including you, have already eaten their shares of this week's oranges! This one's mine!

Sally: Look Philip, I found it first tonight! I picked it up before you! It's mine!

Philip: Sally, I have done much more food shopping than you or anyone else living here for that matter. If anyone deserves that orange, it's me!

Because each is positioned, asserting his or her "right" to the orange, Sally and Philip are not able to work this out themselves. Instead, the conflict escalates uncontrollably without an end in sight.

SOURCE: *THE ORANGE CASE*

This "**Orange Case**" is adapted from Roger Fisher and William Ury with Bruce Patton, editor, *Getting To Yes: Negotiating Agreement Without Giving In* (Boston: Houghton Mifflin, 2011), 57, 73.

Introducing negotiation fundamentals

But what if these roommates could instead say why they wanted the orange—exactly what their interests were? It turns out that Sally wants the orange to squeeze some orange juice, while Philip wants the rind to make a cake. Discovering that each wants a different part of the orange could allow them to focus instead on interests, and reach an agreement themselves.

Whereas negotiations that focused on positions might lead them to compromise and to splitting the orange in half, each roommate could get more when negotiations focused on their interests. In this case, one would get all the juice while the other gets all the rind. Furthermore, by reaching this resolution themselves, these roommates could improve their relationship and make negotiations easier in the future. Many additional benefits are possible when negotiations are based on meeting interests rather than fighting over positions. Both parties can win.

In this chapter, I focus on how to negotiate most effectively. The five principles and practices listed below, adapted from Roger Fisher and William Ury's classic *Getting to Yes*, can help you get results even in the most difficult negotiations.

1. *Focus on interests, not positions*
2. *Reframe, reframe, reframe*
3. *Persuade first and, whenever possible, avoid using threats*
4. *Invent options that may benefit both parties*
5. *Insist on objective criteria*

How conflicts escalate

Most escalations are not sudden. They develop slowly out of minor insults and mounting frustrations in a human relationship. They are a result of misunderstandings and genuinely differing interests that are not handled effectively when they first arise. This is common knowledge. It is also the reason why early intervention can be so beneficial in keeping conflicts contained. By contrast, once a conflict gathers a momentum of its own, relatively few people are willing (or able) to step back and examine its roots to see how they might be untangled.

Psychologist Daniel Dana , a specialist in resolving workplace conflict, proposes a useful system for classifying the levels of conflict we experience. There are "blips," which are difficult moments in a fairly healthy relationship. There are "clashes," which describe more sustained and significant times of discord. And then there are "crises," the acute and dangerous conflicts whose defining characteristic is the instability they bring into the lives of all concerned.

Many crises are born of blips that could have been contained. When a conflict grows serious, it can look as if it will take over the entire stage and rewrite the script of your life. But it is important to remember that the conflict is not all that is going on. It is not even all that's going on in your relationship with your tenant. You can be irritated at the tenant who took your parking space (again!). Yet, you can still find her pleasant enough to talk with. You might be worried that the behavior of teenagers in your building is slipping over the edge and posing a danger to other tenants. At the same time, you can stay friendly with the kids' parents and maybe even have a frank discussion about your concerns with them. While it can

SOURCE: MANAGING DIFFERENCES

Daniel Dana, *Managing Differences: How to Build Better Relationships at Work and Home* (Prairie Village, KS: MTI Publications, 2006).

sometimes be crazy-making, this complexity is actually a plus, because it allows landlords and tenants to find common ground as they work out their differences.

Nevertheless in some disputes, in spite of common ground, a climate of instability eventually sets in. Negotiated agreements break down, not once, but repeatedly. Losses mount beyond an acceptable level. Destructive behaviors may even enter the picture. The main reason for the instability may be a tenant who is chronically incapable of paying the rent, communicating reasonably, treating the premises respectfully, or otherwise complying with the law. Instability may also come from a landlord who cannot maintain a habitable apartment, respect a tenant's privacy, communicate well, or otherwise comply with the law.

To understand how negotiation that emphasizes interests may be used, let's take a dispute I worked on a while back involving Janine, a landlord, and her tenant Philip. Philip and Janine were arguing over including an additional occupant on the lease. Philip wanted to add an additional occupant to reduce the monthly costs-per-tenant for himself and his roommates. Janine was opposed, concerned about wear and tear, extra water use and peaceful enjoyment. Let's discuss this dispute as the five negotiation fundamentals are introduced.

1. Focus on interests, not positions

When Philip and Janine approached me, they did not have any problems articulating their positions and threats. Philip told me, "My roommates and I will move out immediately if we cannot add an additional roommate." Janine told me, "If another roommate is added, I will evict them all." Janine did not want the excess wear and tear, higher water costs, and potential noise that might ensue.

I HAVE ADVISED MY CLIENT NOT TO FETCH ANY BASEBALL WITHOUT A CONTRACT SECURING ONE MILLION OUNCES OF GOURMET DOG FOOD WITH BONUS BELLY-SCRATCHINGS AND THE OPTION TO RENEGOTIATE AFTER FOURTEEN YEARS... DOG YEARS, OF COURSE...

offthemark.com

Positions are what we typically state as our right, what we demand, what "should" be the resolution to the dispute at hand. Threats represent one strategy for influencing your opponent to meet your demands. Janine's position going into the negotiation is: "I won't tolerate any more wear and tear on this apartment. No more roommates!" Janine's threat, that she would evict, provides leverage. Philip's position is "We will add another roommate." His threat is that the three existing roommates would move out if a fourth roommate is not permitted.

Interests, however, are different from positions. Interests are what we want or need. Interests are what truly motivate us. Philip wanted to save money per person and was willing to accept a higher rent overall, knowing each roommate's monthly share would be lower. Janine wanted to reduce wear and tear. She also wanted to reduce turnover and make more money as a result.

To distinguish positions from interests more clearly, take another example. An angry contractor insists he is owed two-thirds of the entire contract although he is only one-quarter of the way through the job. He is ready to walk off the job. "I'm not paying you that amount!" the landlord shouts back. "No way, given your lack of follow-through!" The dispute escalates.

Now, let's roll this dispute back to the point before the threats were hurled and negotiations broke off. What if the landlord discussed his interests,

---

SOURCE: INTERESTS

Fisher and Ury introduce the idea of interest-based negotiation in *Getting to Yes*.

The Good Landlord

namely that he wanted to pay less than this two-thirds sum for the following reasons:

- ❏ The contractor had used lower cost materials than were specified in the contract
- ❏ The landlord, himself, had contributed labor
- ❏ The contractor was behind schedule

The contractor could then agree to a lower amount, but he wanted a more reliable form of payment, namely cash or certified checks instead of personal or business checks.

As the discussion unfolded, moreover, other interests became clear. The landlord could save money on the second and third payments, for instance, by buying the materials himself. By getting the job back on schedule, the contractor regained the landlord's trust and could secure a positive reference from the landlord. By getting at each other's interests, these parties were able to reach a settlement, and a better one at that. The parties avoided escalating the dispute, thus saving money, time, and stress.

When landlords and tenants are able to discuss their interests, in most cases dispute resolution becomes easier and better agreements are possible. Here is a more complete list of the interests of tenants and landlords:

Landlord vs. Tenant interests

Landlord Interests

▲ *Getting the rent, and in a timely fashion*

▲ *Securing reasonable rent increases*

▲ *Accessing the unit reliably*

▲ *Maintaining peaceful enjoyment of the premises*

▲ *Avoiding costly repairs*

▲ *Avoiding costly professionals*

▲ *Successfully screening for and selecting tenants*

▲ *Filling apartments without undue effort*

▲ *Keeping overall costs down*

▲ *Maintaining a good reputation with tenants and neighbors*

▲ *Freeing up time for other pursuits*

▲ *Achieving the self-respect that comes from being an ethical landlord*

Tenant Interests

▲ *Affordable rent*

▲ *Well-maintained unit*

▲ *Security*

▲ *Self-respect that comes from a fair business deal*

▲ *Peaceful enjoyment of the premises*

▲ *Effective communication*

▲ *Prompt and reliable maintenance and repairs*

▲ *A reasonable, flexible response when the tenant falls behind on rent*

▲ *Landlord willingness to work with tenant in the event of other tenancy breaches*

When negotiating, the following two suggestions can help you discuss your interests most effectively.

Make your interests specific: If you want to meet your interests as a landlord, you need to communicate what they are. For example, when you tell your tenant that gaining access to her unit the next evening is necessary in order to fix the toilet, even if it is inconvenient for her, also let her know that the reason you need a specialized contractor that particular evening is because the toilet is leaking through the floor and ruining the ceiling below. Such an explanation will help your tenant better appreciate your interests.

In another example, your tenant may not understand the effect her noise is having on the other tenants in the building. Making your interests specific and communicating them effectively can strengthen your hand.

Focus on the future: You can more effectively satisfy your interests if you can discuss how you want things to be in the future. Rather than to discuss how poorly your tenant managed disposing of the trash last summer, for example, you can remind her how happy you are that she is now handling the trash successfully and that you want this to continue.

2. Reframe, reframe, reframe

When each party pursues only her own interests when negotiating, each party can quickly become locked into rigid positions, making it less likely that agreements can be reached. How can two parties avoid getting locked into rigid positions? Each can assert what she wants until the cows come home, but if both cannot find a way to resolve their differences, the stalemate will keep escalating unless another approach is used.

Reframing can help. Reframing takes the real meaning of what each party is saying and *translates* it into something that can move you forward. Just as a picture frame shapes how a picture is presented, an issue can also be framed. Landlords have a variety of ways that they can reframe problems to make agreements satisfactory to both parties.

How can you reframe the problem to best meet your own interests? If Philip had reframed the problem as an opportunity for Janine to make more money from the deal with less hassle, he might have made more progress. Janine could have reframed it as how to make more money and reduce turnover. If the roommates fighting over the orange, moreover, had named their own interests up front, conflict would have been minimized. One roommate could have had the entire fruit of the orange, while the other the entire rind. Even though landlord-tenant conflicts are not always as resolvable as these examples illustrate, the principles of negotiation, introduced here, are highly applicable.

To reframe a dispute, ask the right questions

The ability to ask the right questions is essential in helping you to reframe disputes and reach your goals. Effective questions open the door to knowledge and understanding, which can lead to skillful negotiation. What if Philip had asked Janine: "How important would additional rent money be for you?" Or, "How much wear and tear can this unit tolerate, Janine, before you need to do an upgrade?" Janine could have asked Philip: "How carefully do you think your roommates could manage yourselves to avoid excess wear and tear?" Or, "If an additional roommate was allowed, how long would you agree to stay in the unit?" Or, "What if you caused damage to the property? Let's discuss this now, in case it were to happen." Asking these questions can turn the parties toward meeting their interests.

Finding the questions that can resolve the underlying issues is the essence of reframing. Try this out: Imagine if you could press a magic button and get any piece of information you want, what would you want to know? The answer will help you compose the right questions.

3. Persuade first and, whenever possible, avoid using threats

Even your best efforts at reframing may leave you short if you do not take the next step toward closing the deal with your tenant. When differences arise, trying to resolve them first by persuasion can not only enhance your relationship—it can also save you money, time, and stress. Trying to meet your tenant's needs as well as your own will undoubtedly test your communication skills, but the potential benefits will likely be worth it.

Emphasize warnings over threats

In seeking to persuade your tenant as a first step, you can benefit enormously by emphasizing negotiation over threats or litigation. You can

provide incentives to talk about each of your interests, including the value of reaching a (legally) well-informed agreement without legal counsel.

There is a subtle distinction that can make an enormous difference if your goal is to emphasize persuasion over coercion. This is the distinction between a warning and a threat. In common usage, there is often little difference. Legally, however, the meanings are worlds apart. Consider these subtly different statements and their not-so-subtle differences in effect:

What is a warning?

A warning communicates that negative consequences will inevitably happen from certain actions, and penalties are provided by the law in the case of proven violations.

Example: Warning: "According to the law, I am allowed to enter your unit to bring it up to code, providing I get your permission, but you need to be reasonable in allowing me access. Here are some possible times we could schedule the plumber. What is best for you? I want to talk this out to avoid having to use legal procedures to gain access."

What is a threat?

A threat expresses your intention to bring those consequences about and strongly implies a withdrawal of cooperation.

Example: Threat: "I have a right to fix my building, and you must give me access. The plumber is scheduled for 8:00 a.m. tomorrow. If you don't let him in, I'll have to evict you."

To inform a tenant about possible legal consequences without making a full-blown threat is one of the true arts of being a successful landlord.

Coercive vs. persuasive conversation

Instead of treating a negotiation as a contest between enemies, try considering it as a problem to be jointly solved. Let's look at the difference between a coercive versus a persuasive approach on a nonpayment situation.

SOURCE: **PERSUADE FIRST**

The ideas in this section are adapted from Fisher and Ury, *Getting to Yes.*

A coercive conversation

The following conversation, on the subject of rent, illustrates the coercive approach.

Tenant: Hello, Steve. What's up?

Landlord: Hi, John. Where's my rent? It's the ninth already.

Tenant: Look, Steve. I'm not talking rent with you. I just called the building inspector to come by tomorrow to cite this unit. You have hardly maintained this place since I moved in.

Landlord: What do you mean, calling the inspector in when I haven't heard any concerns from you for months? You owe me $3,000! Pay it now or I'll evict you!

Tenant: Look, I can avoid paying you for the next year, given these code violations. You just don't care, Steve. I won't pay a dime until you fix this place up. I've also got an advocate working with me who's ready to fight.

Landlord: Look, John. You told me when you first moved in that the place was fine and you really wanted a lower rent. I had the heating situation to respond to, but no other work was needed. Now you're changing your tune.

Tenant: You don't have any choice, Steve. I've got the inspector coming tomorrow, and the city will make sure this unit is fixed up!

Landlord: I can evict you if I need to, John. I don't think any court would take your claims seriously. And when this is all over, you'll have to move and at the next place you will pay twice what your rent is here.

What was said:	Coercive tactic:
▲ *You don't care*	▲ *Personal attack*
▲ *I won't pay a dime until you fix it*	▲ *Treat negotiation as a contest*
▲ *I just called in the inspector*	▲ *Commit to adversarial actions early*
▲ *Pay it now or I'll evict you*	▲ *Narrow the options to either/or*
▲ *I've got an advocate working for me*	▲ *Try to break the opponent's will*
▲ *When this is all over, you'll have to move and at the next place you will be paying twice the amount of rent*	▲ *Worsen tenant's walk-away position*

A persuasive conversation

For every coercive tactic, however, there is an alternative, one that can meet both your interests and your tenants' as well. See how things could have developed:

Tenant: Hello, Steve.

Landlord: Hi, John. I'm calling you about the rent. It's the ninth day of the month and I haven't received it yet. We've got the previous two months unpaid as well. I know there are some repair issues to discuss which I'm willing to do, but I would first like to understand your situation with paying the rent. How's it been going?

Tenant: It's going all right.

Landlord: Well I'd like to figure this out together if we can. I know you've been upset by some things, and I think if we can discuss it, we'll have a better chance of making progress here.

Tenant: Thanks for asking. Well things are tough. And when you put it all together, I just haven't been able to get the rent to you.

The Good Landlord

Landlord: What's been going on?

Tenant: I've been cut back to half-time in my job, which has reduced my income, so things are quite tight right now. I'm also aware that there are some things that need repair in the unit. I've considered calling an inspector, but I don't need to push this given that the rent has been reasonable. I really want to be able to stay here, Steve.

Landlord: I understand that things are tight. Sounds challenging. I do appreciate your understanding that I don't have an unlimited budget right now. What are you doing to try to increase your income?

Tenant: I'm looking to supplement with various part-time jobs, but don't have anything yet. I've updated my resume and have my cousin, who's a career coach, helping me. But finding a job is rough going at the moment. I expect I'll find some work within a couple months, though.

Landlord: I can appreciate the effort it takes. What can you do, though, to make up this income?

Tenant: Maybe I could help you make some of these repairs, in exchange for the rent. I would definitely be interested and have done a lot of carpentry work as you know, Steve.

Landlord (*thinks for a moment and then replies*): Yes, I have seen your work and know you've got good carpentry skills. I could offer you some maintenance and repair projects in lieu of half the rent due for the month. You would pay half a month's rent for each of the next two months. I know you've expressed interest in this before.

Tenant: That sounds great, Steve. This barter arrangement can make a big difference for me. Thanks! And please know I'm open to doing this barter arrangement over the long term if it's helpful.

Landlord: I'm open to this barter I've described but will need to resume charging the entire rent after this arrangement ends, given my own financial limitations. If new work becomes available and your work is good, I'll consider extending it, but I have others who I may resume working with, so please do not count on it.

Tenant: I understand. Thank you! I think you'll like my work. Also, if I were to work for you in the future, there may be energy-saving projects we discover which would save you money while also preventing further deterioration in the building.

The coercive and persuasive scripts above provide examples of language that can produce success whether tenants move out or stay. You hold a lot of cards in your relationship with tenants, among them, the power to evict or raise the rent. Remembering this can provide the peace of mind needed to play these cards effectively.

Two tips for avoiding a coercive conversation

Consult before you decide

In most cases, talking over significant decisions with your tenants before you make them can be helpful. Whether you are deciding to raise the rent, replace the floors, fix a toilet, or pursue eviction, you will lose little and gain much by consulting tenants beforehand. Consulting first does mean you may need to consider reasonable changes to your plan, however. By consulting your tenants beforehand and being willing to be persuaded, though, you also

The Good Landlord

Consider the benefits of the persuasive approaches that were used

---

Attack the problem (not the person)

What was said:

Landlord: How's it been going? I would first like to understand your situation with paying the rent.

Tenant: I'm also aware that there are some things that need repair in the unit. I've considered calling an inspector, but I don't need to push this given that the rent has been reasonable. I really want to be able to stay here, Steve.

Express appreciation

What was said:

Landlord: I do appreciate your understanding that I don't have an unlimited budget right now.

Tenant: Thanks for asking.... This barter arrangement can make a big difference for me.... I understand....

Explore interests

What was said:

Tenant: Maybe I could help you make some of these repairs in exchange for the rent.

Landlord: For the next two months, I could offer you some maintenance and repair projects as a barter in lieu of half the rent due for the month.

Tenant: And please know I'm open to doing this barter arrangement over the long term if it's helpful.

Try to persuade based on what is fair

What was said:

Landlord: If new work becomes available and your work is good, I'll consider extending it, but I have others who I may resume working with, so please do not count on it.

Improve your walk-away position

What was said:

Tenant: I think you'll like my work. Also, if I were to work for you in the future, there may be energy-saving projects we discover which would save you money while also preventing further deterioration in the building.

---

stand to gain. You are likely to secure their cooperation, carry out a plan that both you and your tenant can buy into, and strengthen your future relationship.

Consulting beforehand does not also mean you have to cede control over decision-making. I am not suggesting that you give your tenant veto power over your plan. Perhaps your tenant prefers a beige tile on the bathroom floor, though, which might not be a problem. Perhaps she wants a different bathroom lighting arrangement that is less expensive and also fine with you. Allowing your tenants to have input in these kinds of situations can add value without your losing control over the things you care most about.

Your tenant may request things, however, which you won't agree to provide, such as new kitchen cabinets, new windows, or a new stove. Whether or not the tenant agrees with your plan, making her aware beforehand of what you can and cannot do will help your cause.

Show your reasoning

When you show your reasoning, you will also be likely to get better results. Let's illustrate this with the following scenario. Your tenant is arguing that her **defenses and counterclaims**, based on violation of state habitability codes, equal the three months of rent she owes. You could oppose her with comments like these: "There's no way your rent abatements will offset anything near what you owe! I can evict you easily! Why don't you pay your rent now so we can resolve this?"

Or, you could try to persuade her by showing your reasoning. You could show that:

- ❐ You responded quickly when informed about code-related repair issues, thus preventing the need for rent abatements. You also have a well-organized paper trail to back up your timely response.

The Good Landlord

❑ The code issues she raises, based on your own analysis, are not significant, and would only allow for a small percentage per day off the rent.

❑ Your own review of possible rent abatements leads you to believe a maximum of 15% of the monthly rent would be abated for the time in question.

You could then:

❑ Negotiate a resolution with your tenant, thus avoiding a trial.

❑ Offer a 20% abatement if you can resolve this issue yourselves. You'll take a payment plan for getting the back rent provided the case is entered into court as an enforceable agreement. This would include getting a complete withdrawal of claims or actions.

For each point you make, you can invite your tenant to disagree with you, listening for his reasoning. The goal is to avoid making threats while getting your tenant to agree with your conclusions by showing your reasoning.

To achieve this goal does not call for magic, but requires learning a few lessons offered in this book. The Good Landlord approach to eviction, presented in the next chapter, illustrates how a more reasoned approach can help tenants to follow your plan.

LEGAL INFO: DEFENSES AND COUNTERCLAIMS

Under Massachusetts law, if a tenant files a timely Answer to a landlord's eviction case, he can make both defenses and counterclaims to his landlord's suit. His **defenses** are legal arguments about why he, not the landlord, should win the case. His **counterclaims** are money damages he may have against the landlord, which may also cause the landlord to lose the case. See the discussion on Answer and Request for Discovery, page 79.

4. Invent options that benefit both parties

You probably know from your own experience that when each person argues his own view of the problem, it is easy for disputes to escalate. Each states his position. Alternative views are not entertained. The dispute continues and is likely to escalate.

On the other hand, the idea of *inventing options before deciding* may not be so easy, even if the advantages seem obvious. Inventing options does not come naturally. In most people's minds, inventing is not part of the negotiating process. To invent options before deciding suggests that landlords separate the act of inventing from the act of committing to a solution. This involves expanding the possible resolutions instead of insisting on the "right" one.

SOURCE: INVENTING OPTIONS

Adapted from "Inventing options for mutual gain" in Fisher and Ury, *Getting to Yes*, 60.

The Good Landlord

Consider the differences between declaring the "right" solution and generating different options on the following two issues:

Of course emergencies occur in which landlords need access immediately,

Gaining access to make repairs

The "right" solution	Different options
Landlord: I must have access tomorrow at 2 p.m.	**Landlord:** What if I have access with 24-hour notice whether or not you're in the unit, unless for exceptional circumstances.
	Tenant: If you communicate with me regarding when I am home or not, you can have access even sooner than 24 hours, particularly for emergencies.
	Tenant: If you can wait just four days, I'll be away for one week during which you can have all the access you want.

Paying the back rent

The "right" solution	Different options
Landlord: I must be paid back all the rent in two weeks or I'll evict you.	**Landlord:** I can accept rent at different times of the month based on when you get your paychecks.
	Landlord: If I get your current rent every month along with some arrearage, and the agreement is entered as enforceable by the courts, then I can extend the payment plan longer.

despite tenant objections, and negotiation is not possible. In most cases, however, when landlords and tenants invent options before deciding, they can consider the costs and benefits of each option before deciding which one to agree to. The parties can then settle on a solution that both prefer while strengthening their relationship as well. The benefits to both are potentially enormous.

SOURCE: *INSIST ON OBJECTIVE CRITERIA*

This principle is adapted from Fisher and Ury's: *Getting to Yes*, 81.

5. Insist on objective criteria

However well you negotiate, there will always remain issues over which landlords and tenants disagree. Whereas the landlord wants only three occupants to live in a unit, the tenant wants four. Whereas the landlord wants to be able to gain access as needed, the tenant wants to restrict access to certain weekdays and never on weekends. There is no lack of possible differences.

It is quite common for people to use positional bargaining to resolve their differences, each stating their own demands while opposing the other's. We tend to tell people what we are willing or unwilling to accept. For example, a landlord I worked with insisted that he had maintained the unit 100% and was demanding 100% rent payment now. His tenant insisted that rent abatements were in order and refused to pay anything higher than 35% of the rent owed. Built into each side's position are criteria each sees as fair. In this case, the landlord insisted that he maintained the unit well, according to building codes, so the tenant should pay the back rent now. The tenant, however, raised defenses, arguing that she should be awarded abatements based on **warranty of habitability** claims, namely that:

- ❐ The unit needed code-required repairs;
- ❐ The landlord had not responded to these repair issues in a timely fashion;
- ❐ The landlord had been properly notified;
- ❐ The landlord had not been denied access; and
- ❐ The tenant had not caused the problems himself.

▌ **LEGAL INFO: *WARRANTY OF HABITABILITY***

The Massachusetts Supreme Judicial Court ruled that when a landlord fails to maintain a dwelling in a habitable condition, a tenant can properly withhold a portion of the rent from the date the landlord has notice of this breach of the **warranty of habitability** (M.G.L. c. 239 sec. 8A). Withholding rent can be a useful tool for tenants to force repairs, but it is a serious step and should be dealt with carefully. As emphasized in this book, tenants should first appeal to their landlord in writing to make the (continued)

Now the tenant was ready to go to court. If the parties could reach resolution themselves, it would depend on successfully using the warranty of habitability as objective criteria for deciding what rent abatements would be acceptable. The parties worked it out.

In another example, a tenant who called me was linking her asthma condition to excessive mold in the bathroom. The landlord, who I also spoke with, thought other factors were more important. The tenant wanted to reduce the back rent owed because she had lived with this problem for too long. Without an agreement over which methods to use, the parties were likely to continue fighting over whose view was right.

If the landlord and tenant could agree to utilize fair and objective criteria to determine a possible rent reduction, however, each party could benefit more. Here are some possible methods I offered for reaching a fair resolution:

- ❒ Conduct a test to determine how much mold is present.
- ❒ Examine research that identifies general sources of mold, whether this tenant's primary exposure is from the bathroom, and for how long the exposure may have occurred.
- ❒ Determine how much mold exposure (dose, length) would lead one to become asthmatic.

Using any or all of these methods might allow the parties to narrow their differences and reach agreement themselves. The parties agreed to do a mold test, worked out a plan for removing the mold, and agreed to a modest rent abatement.

LEGAL INFO: ***WARRANTY OF HABITABILITY, CONTINUED***

necessary repairs. As well, tenants will often contact their local board of health to inspect the apartment for health code violations. Tenants must be current in their rent up until the time of the problem, and the unsanitary conditions should be such that they do not require the apartment to be vacated. If initial efforts to secure repairs do not work, a tenant may then write to his landlord informing him that she will be withholding rent, making sure to specify her reasoning for doing so. Deciding how much to withhold is individual to the situation of the tenant (e.g., the cost for loss of heat or other major inconvenience). The tenant may then pay only the fair rent for their unit given its defective condition. For more information, see pages 50 and 199.

Although individual judges can interpret the law differently, landlords and tenants will reach better agreements when they can negotiate effectively before trial. Insisting on objective criteria, and using the negotiation principles presented here, can make an enormous difference.

Commonly applied criteria used by landlords to resolve landlord-tenant disputes include:

▲ *Market value of the property, i.e., what is being charged for rent or for sale for similar buildings*

▲ *Precedent (how similar cases have been decided)*

▲ *What a judge would decide*

▲ *How relevant laws, policies and regulations apply*

▲ *Efficiency (saving money, saving time)*

▲ *Scientific, medical, environmental, or other standards*

In the next chapter, we will discuss how these negotiation fundamentals can be used to address the issue of eviction directly.

The Good Landlord

Questions for reflection: Getting what you need: Negotiation fundamentals

---

1. How would you characterize your negotiating style? Are you more adversarial? More accommodating? Do you try to avoid conflict?

    _____

    _____

    _____

    _____

    _____

2. Do you typically try at first to work things out with your tenants, using coercion or threats as a last resort?

    _____

    _____

    _____

    _____

    _____

3. What may be difficult about trying to work things out with your tenant?

    _____

    _____

    _____

    _____

    _____

4. Look back at a conflict you had with a tenant. In what ways could you have restored your relationship so as to continue as a "good" landlord?

    _____

    _____

    _____

    _____

    _____

11

The Good Landlord
approach to eviction:
Two-Track response

Remember Joe and Maria in Chapter 6, the
landlords whose relationship with their tenants
turned sour? That relationship didn't fall apart
all at once. For a while, there was euphoria, with
a true spirit of collaboration, on both sides. Then
there was comfort and habitual good will. Still later,
there was politeness, then occasional aloofness,
and finally increasing discomfort. Only after many
months did the situation deteriorate to the point
where communication was impossible.

If Joe and Maria had applied the skills discussed in the previous chapters, they might have been able to keep the situation under control. And if they needed to pursue eviction to resolve the dispute, they could have employed alternatives to all-out warfare. These alternatives are the subject of this chapter.

When eviction is the best option

The habits contained in an unconditionally constructive strategy, as identified in Chapters 8, 9 and 10, are powerful in solving the landlord's daily problems. Whether you are securing access, negotiating regarding pets, or raising the rent, this strategy can carry you far, even with the most difficult tenants. It does not rely on the other side's goodwill, but instead encourages effective problem-solving and the building of a mutually beneficial relationship even when your tenant is obstinate. Following these habits can also keep tenants in negotiating mode when disputes escalate.

When eviction cases escalate, however, the use of legal rights becomes inevitable. After weeks or months of unproductive conversations over paying the back rent, a landlord may take the first legal step by serving an eviction notice. A tenant may respond in self defense by calling in the building inspector and asserting her rights. The landlord pursues access. The tenant denies it. The case escalates.

When legal procedures begin, there is a quantum shift in the conversation between the parties in the conflict. Instead of focusing on interests and desires, the discussion turns toward rights and sources of power. Tensions can skyrocket. Your dispute can easily and unexpectedly spiral out of control at a time when you very much want it resolved—before it goes to court.

Introducing Two-Track response

The use of the Two-Track Response (Two-Track) offers the possibility of using negotiation to avoid disputes from escalating in the first place. Two-Track can save valuable time and money by helping landlords reach agreements on their eviction cases before trial day. And Two-Track can help you know when and how to evict your tenant when needed. This chapter will describe how to pursue Two-Track successfully. Specifically, I will show you how to negotiate with your tenant (Track One), as you proceed toward court (Track Two).

It is commonly assumed that when legal action starts, communication stops. Not so with Two-Track. It becomes possible to communicate

Go to where the money is

My dad's approach to collecting money has inspired me since I was young. Dad was able to collect money no matter what circumstances arose. He confidently described his journeys from New Jersey to central Long Island, to small warehouses, garages, or other places where there was someone ready to pay him.

He wasn't afraid. He would call his customers several times, write letters, knock on doors, start legal procedures, and continue pestering them, politely but firmly, to complete the business at hand. "Go to where the money is. Be persistent," my dad would remind me. Whether in regard to collecting debts or pursuing other tasks that required overcoming resistance, he would state: "And don't be proud."

To this day, I often find the courage to approach tenants when they owe me rent by remembering the lessons offered by my dad's experiences.

Although your tenants may respond to your initiative by becoming more tense and defensive, collecting rent is your right and you should pursue it! Find a way to ask for what is owed you. And be persistent!

effectively as legal steps are taken, with the goal of reaching a win-win agreement for all involved.

Ingredients for success

When you are functioning in an unconditionally constructive mode, the goal is to rely on the legal system as little as possible, while using it to protect your rights. This does not mean that you sacrifice your rights, now or in the future, for the sake of accommodation. It also does not mean that you turn up the heat without first establishing the strategic value of doing so, and without making sure your actions are driven by *principles* rather than *panic*. Wise use of the legal process is a core element for using the Good Landlord approach to eviction. The Good Landlord approach depends on this and other ingredients as well. As a good landlord, you should:

1. ***Match your response to the conflict***. Fit the forum to the fuss. Match whatever process is used—informal talks, negotiation, mediation and/or litigation—to the conflict at hand. If the fuss is less about concrete results and more about getting some acknowledgment for the efforts you have been expending, maybe the forum should be a more personal, low-key conversation. (But again, don't expect appreciation.) If your interest is to work out a plan for the tenant to resume paying rent while you make needed repairs, the appropriate forum may be a mediation session, with each party informed of his or her rights. If you have done everything you can to resolve the conflict before seeing the judge, the appropriate forum is then litigation.

   Refer to Comfort, stretch and panic zones, page 137

2. ***Stabilize your legal situation as you resolve the dispute, whether or not you are preparing for trial***. Knowing that tenants have strong legal protections and may use them liberally, you should first resolve your own legal vulnerabilities, if any. You should then, in the most systematic fashion possible, pursue your rights as you negotiate.

   Refer to Express appreciation, page 142

The Good Landlord

3. *Help your tenant to regain stability without sacrificing your own stability*. This can be an important way to reduce conflict. Whether through professionals or your own efforts, identifying and pursuing resources (benefits, services or programs, and the professional support and supervision needed, such as advocacy, mentoring or case management) can significantly help your tenant and thus you to become more stable. Helping your tenant helps you!

4. *Make the best use of professionals*. This involves knowing when it is best to involve an attorney or other professional, and how much help is needed. In many cases, when you are legally well informed, you may want to unbundle your legal needs. If the case escalates, you can always increase your reliance on your attorney.

Refer to Consider unbundling your legal services, page 79

The Good Landlord approach to eviction: The three stages

Stage	Good Landlord approach	Timetable	Professional assistance
Stage 1: Informal agreements	▲ Pursues informal agreements early on. ▲ Puts little or nothing in writing. ▲ Follows through informally. ▲ Refines the plan once or twice if tenant needs to renegotiate. ▲ Continues to monitor but doesn't go too long before going to Stage #2. ▲ Does not serve formal notices at this stage.	2–25 days after breach of tenancy	Landlord takes the lead with property manager or other professional as backup. Informal assistance from lawyer, mediator, or other professional.
Stage 2: Two-Track response	▲ Serves Notice to Terminate Tenancy while also informing the tenant in writing that landlord wants to continue to negotiate and reach an agreement if possible. ▲ Continues to pursue an agreement with tenant, which can happen right through trial day. ▲ Serves Summons to start court eviction process. ▲ Plans to have any agreements reached at this stage entered into the court record as an enforceable agreement for judgment. ▲ Prepares for trial including responding to any and all legal procedures.	10–45 days after breach (may vary from state to state)	Landlord and/or property manager, with help from lawyer, mediator, or other professional.
Stage 3: Trial day	▲ Appears in court. ▲ Approaches tenant, if interested, to continue negotiations on their own. ▲ Uses court mediation services if available. ▲ Submits the agreement, if reached, to the judge, as an enforceable action of the court. ▲ Appears before judge if no agreement is reached on trial day.	According to timing of court procedures	Property manager can accompany landlord. Lawyer often is needed.

Moving from Stage 1 to Stage 2: The hardest step

How might this three-stage Good Landlord approach improve your ability to resolve a problem with nonpayment? Landlords can pursue Stage 1, informal agreements, for a round or two, which can lead some tenants to pay up. Other tenants, unfortunately, will not pay up, and may use this stage to avoid making these payments indefinitely. And many landlords will let this stage drag on for many months without going to Stage 2. They do this because their tenants promise time and time again that this time they will follow through—this time they really mean it. These promises can ease landlord concerns about getting paid. Landlords also figure they can avoid having to go to court and ultimately evict, which can be costly and time consuming. But there can be trouble ahead.

If landlords do not monitor these informal agreements, and they do not move to Stage 2, many nonpayment cases will escalate indefinitely until they reach a breaking point. At this breaking point, when landlords realize further action is needed, they are facing the beginning of a difficult road ahead, not the end. ***This breaking point can be quite explosive, landlords, so, beware! You may feel so angry, betrayed, and revengeful that you leap from Stage 1 right over Stage 2 to Stage 3!*** You may feel you have no choice but to proceed to court no matter what the cost.

Refer to page 238, Eviction procedures

When disputes escalate like this, each side begins to assert its rights more aggressively and to make legal threats. For example, your tenant is more likely to claim that

- ❏ You have gained access illegally
- ❏ You have mismanaged the security deposit
- ❏ You have violated her peaceful enjoyment rights by allowing other tenants in the building to be disruptive

❏ You have discriminated on the basis of age, source of income, marital status or other category

❏ You have retaliated in response to your tenant asserting her rights

Once legal procedure begins, absent early intervention, the case will undoubtedly escalate. And then, after losing months of back rent, landlords now additionally have to respond to tenants' legal defenses, making the landlord more likely to retaliate and seek revenge. *Many landlords face sleepless nights, angry that they did not take legal action earlier.* But legal procedures will need to run their course, requiring ongoing professional assistance, likely delays, and continuing uncertainty over the outcome.

Two caveats

Number 1: I am not advocating that landlords avoid going to court when tenants need to be evicted. The Good Landlord approach to eviction described here, however, can help landlords pursue faster, cheaper and often better resolutions as a first step, using court proceedings as needed.

Number 2: There will also be cases, inevitably, where tenants lead with their legal defenses despite how well landlords use the practices offered in this book. Tenants will often succeed more against landlords who don't use these practices, however. Using the practices in this book makes your success more likely. These practices can make a difference.

Discussion and sample conversations

How might discussions go in each of these three stages? Below are guidelines and sample discussions you can use for each of the three stages.

Stage 1: Informal agreements

- ❏ Landlords should start this process a few days after the tenant falls behind in rent.
- ❏ Landlords first need to make contact with their tenants.
- ❏ Landlords should listen to their tenants and be open to reasonable, timely payment plans, ideally suggested by the tenants.
- ❏ Landlords do not need to put these plans in writing, at least at first, unless the tenant requests it.

When tenants themselves suggest the payment terms, while things are still casual and nothing is in writing, compliance is most likely. The tenant gets to control the process, suggest the plan, look good, and save face.

First conversation: *March 5*

Landlord (Susan)	Tenant (David)
How are you, David? Hope all's well with you and your family. I was just calling to discuss the rent for this month—$1,050.	Yes, I've been meaning to call you, Susan, but it's really been busy around here. I'm sorry. It's been rough financially but here's what I can do. I can pay you when I get paid. I can pay you $525 on March 10th and the rest on March 20th. How would that be?

Landlord	Tenant
I can work with that. Let's stay in touch. I understand that things have been hard for you, and I'm glad we have a plan. I look forward to this working out.	Thanks, Susan. I'm also looking forward to this working out.

Second conversation: *March 12*

Landlord (Susan)	Tenant (David)
Hi David. I was just checking back with you. We had discussed that you make a payment on March 10th, which was due two days ago. I haven't received it yet. How's it going?	Oh yeah. I'm glad you're checking back. Sorry about that, Susan. It's been rough, but now I know better what I'm able to do. What if I give you one-third of the rent instead, right now. Here's $350. (*Hands over a money order.*) I can then give you another $175 in four days, on March 16th. That will only be half of the $1,050 due, but I hope you'll work with me on this.

Landlord	Tenant
That sounds okay (taking $350). Thank you. So you're saying I can expect $175 on the sixteenth?	Yes, I can pay that on the 16th of March. I know I also need to resolve the other half with you.

The Good Landlord

Second conversation: March 12

Landlord (Susan)	Tenant (David)
That's okay. Let's write this up, though. I also need to take another step which can be helpful as well. If I don't get the $175 by March 16th as you've stated, I will need to serve the nonpayment notice. I would serve it expecting not to go any further, but for both of us to have options if this payment plan doesn't work. I will still work with you as you continue to catch up, David. If you can't follow the plan, we can both take advantage of the court process. Each of us can make use of our legal rights.	I would rather you not serve me a notice, but I do understand. I want this to work. I want to stay here. After paying $175 on March 16th, I will make payments of $200 on March 21st and March 28th, and then a final payment for $125 for March on April 3rd. Then, if you agreed, I will pay my April rent in three equal payments of $350 on April 10, 17th and 24th totaling $1,050. Would you agree to this?

Landlord	Tenant
I will agree to this and let's write up the plan to make it easier to follow.	Thank you.

March 12th payment plan

Date	Arrearage	Status	Current Rent
March 12	$350	Paid	
March 16th	$175	Pending	
March 21st	$200	Pending	
March 28th	$200	Pending	
April 3rd	$125	Pending	
April 10th		Pending	$350 (April rent)
April 17th		Pending	$350 (April rent)
April 24th		Pending	$350 (April rent)
Totals:	$1,050		$1,050

Stage 2: Two-Track response

- ❏ The tenant paid $100 instead of the $175 due on March 16th.
- ❏ The landlord begins legal procedures—serving the nonpayment notice—while continuing to negotiate. Getting eviction procedures underway establishes time limits for moving dispute resolution forward while the landlord pursues a court-enforceable agreement.
- ❏ Pursuing the two tracks—negotiation and legal—can compel the parties to reach an agreement without landlords losing any time if negotiations break down or agreements are not met. You can remind tenants who do not want to proceed toward court that you can put the court date off, perhaps multiple times as allowed by the designated court, provided the overdue rent is being paid as agreed.

First conversation: March 17

Landlord (Susan)	Tenant (David)
Hi David. How are you?	Hi Susan. I'm okay. What's up?
Landlord	**Tenant**
Firstly, I wanted to thank you for paying the $100. As I had mentioned on March 12th, though, I will be serving the nonpayment notice as I received $100, not the $175, by the 16th. Please expect that notice tomorrow. I remain open to working together, though, and expect to reach our own agreement without going to court. We can use the court procedure as a last resort. You have rights as do I.	I don't think it's necessary to start the court process, Susan. I've been straightforward about my situation. I do have some repair issues I could raise if this goes further. I can catch up with the rent if you continue to work with me.
Landlord	**Tenant**
I appreciate what you're saying, David, and expect that we won't need to go to court. Having the court process, however, can benefit both of us. I want to keep working with you so that you can make the rent payments in a timely fashion.	I certainly don't want to go to court on this. Let's get this plan down on paper so I know what needs to happen when.
Landlord	**Tenant**
Let's do that.	

The Good Landlord

Tenant and landlord work out a new, written payment schedule, adding $25 to each future arrearage payment—$225 on March 21st, $225 on March 28th and $150 on April 3rd.

March 17th payment plan

Date	Arrearage	Status	Current Rent
March 12	$350	Paid	
March 16th	$100	Paid	
March 21st	$225	Pending	
March 28th	$225	Pending	
April 3rd	$150	Pending	
April 10th		Pending	$350
April 17th		Pending	$350
April 24th		Pending	$350
Totals:	$1,050		$1,050

Second conversation: April 5

Landlord (Susan)	Tenant (David)
Hi David.	Hi Susan.

Landlord	Tenant
I was calling to check back with you. According to my records, you paid me $100 instead of the $175 on the 16th. You then paid $150 instead of $225 for both the March 21st and March 28th payments. And you didn't make the $150 payment due April 3rd. My figures show $300 owed still for March plus $1,050 for April, totaling $1,350. Is that what you figured?	Yes, that figure is right. I had a couple expenses I didn't expect which changed my budget.

Landlord	Tenant
I still expect we can work this out, David, and I did, as I had mentioned, serve the Eviction Summons and Complaint last week. What if we get a new payment schedule down on paper, which could lead to putting off the trial date if we would like.	I'm quite aware of your court application. I am planning on filing my Answer and Discovery next Monday so I can assert my legal defenses and postpone the case for two weeks.

Landlord	Tenant
You mentioned a few days ago that you could raise repair issues. Can you tell me which repairs you're considering raising? Perhaps we can discuss your concerns here and work out an agreement.	I think you'd appreciate, Susan, that I should receive a rent abatement for the time that the hot water tank wasn't replaced immediately, and when the roof leak wasn't repaired while you were away. And I have three other repair issues for which I am requesting rent abatements. I had a lawyer help me determine how much of a rent abatement I should get. I have a paper trail showing when I didn't hear back from you.

Landlord	Tenant
Perhaps you could win some rent abatements, but I don't know. Can you tell me more about the repair issues? How much do you think you would get?	Why should I discuss this here? I'm going to present this to the judge, which could lead to your case being dismissed. What's in it for me to talk about this right now? I'm also considering requesting triple (treble) damages under **Chapter 93A** (the **Consumer Protection Act**) because after you were notified that there were code violations, you still didn't make timely repairs.

▓ LEGAL INFO: *CHAPTER 93A (THE CONSUMER PROTECTION ACT)*

In Massachusetts, the **Consumer Protection Act**, **M.G.L. Chapter 93A**, can apply in certain situations to landlord-tenant disputes. An unhappy tenant sometimes will include a Chapter 93A claim in his answers and counterclaims to an eviction proceeding. Chapter 93A covers "unfair or deceptive practices," including those by landlords. These practices may include building and safety code violations, retaliation against tenants, interfering with a tenant's quiet enjoyment of his apartment, refusing to make requested repairs, improper handling of security deposits, and similar claims. If a tenant is able to prove a 93A claim, a court may award attorney's fees and triple the amount of the proven damages (called treble damages). Generally, owner-occupiers of two-family buildings are exempt from 93A claims.

The Good Landlord

Landlord	Tenant
I don't believe the judge will award you treble damages, David. I do have my own paper trail documenting my good faith efforts to find contractors, secure access and so on, and the time delays were not significant. I am willing, though, to consider offsetting rent owed due to your abatement claims. What if you provide more information for me to consider?	Here are my abatement claims based on the $1,050 per month rent. (*He reviews the specifics.*)

Code violation claims

Repair issue	For how many days did the code violations go unfixed?	Proposed rent abatement (Rent per month = $1,050) (Rent per day = $35)
Roof leak	28 days	20% per day x 28 days = $7.00 x 28 = $196
Drafty windows with gaps	84 days	5% per day x 84 days = $1.75 per day x 84 = $147
Hot water tank replacement	7 days	33% per day x 7 days = 11.66 x 7 = $81.62
Linoleum torn up in bathroom	20 days	5% per day x 20 days = $1.75 x 20 = $35.00
Cracked plaster walls in bedroom	60 days	5% per day x 60 days = $1.75 x 60 = $105.00
Total		**$564.62**

Landlord (Susan)	Tenant (David)
What if I give you $250 as a rent abatement? That would leave $1,100 owed instead of $1,350. I think this is fair given that I have responded reasonably to your repair requests and most of these issues were relatively minor.	My abatement claims add up to $564.62. And that amount would be much higher if triple damages were awarded. I really think $500 is a reasonable amount for a rent abatement. That would leave me owing $850 for April which I could pay by the end of June. I would also like you to repair my bedroom ceiling which has stains and is buckling due to the roof leak.

Second conversation: April 5, continued

Landlord (Susan)	Tenant (David)
I would agree to $350 as a rent abatement. That would leave $1,000 of arrearage for April. I can do the ceiling repair within two weeks.	I can agree to a $425 rent abatement, which would leave me owing $925. If agreeable, I would pay $525 by April 15th, then pay my rent for May, then pay the remaining $400 in two installments—$200 by May 10th and $200 by June 10th. Waiting until the 10th of each month to complete these payments would be very helpful for my cash flow.
Landlord	**Tenant**
Let's go with the $425 rent abatement, leaving $925 owed for April. And I agree to your proposed payment plan. We can write this up as a court enforceable agreement and present it to the judge next week for approval when we are scheduled to appear. I would also like to add that this agreement would settle any and all claims or actions either of us may have or has had against the other up to the present. You can't cite any more code issues from the past, but of course I remain responsible to make code-related repairs in the future. Also, in our agreement, you would need to make your rent payments due for the current month before monies would be credited to back rent. For example, you would need to pay the complete rent for May 1st before I would credit your May 10th payment of $200 to the arrearage. And if you don't make that $200 payment by May 10th, I would be able to get an eviction order immediately. That's how the court process works.	Okay. I agree.

The Good Landlord

District Court Department
Trial Court

Summary Process Docket #_____

Susan Jones   )
Plaintiff   )
v.   )   **AGREEMENT FOR JUDGMENT**
David Doe   )
Defendant   )

We, the parties, understand that we have certain rights and obligations that cannot be changed by a written agreement. We understand that we have entered into this agreement voluntarily. The undersigned parties agree to the following facts and enter into the following agreement as a resolution to their case.

1. Agreed upon rent for the unit is $1,050 per month.
2. The defendant owes $925 representing rent for April, 2015.
3. Judgment for possession of the premises is entered for the plaintiff.
4. Issuance of writ of execution shall be stayed pursuant to the following payment plan.

Date Rent	Arrearage	Current
April 15th	$525	
May 1st		$1,050
May 10th	$200	
June 1st		$1,050
June 10th	$200	
Totals:	$925	$2,100

   Provided the defendant follows this payment plan, this Summary Process case shall be dismissed on June 10th and the defendant's tenancy shall be reinstated.

5. For each month in which an arrearage payment is due, monies must first be paid for the rent currently due for that month before monies can be applied to the arrearage payment due.
6. If there is a violation of this agreement by the defendant, the plaintiff may file with this court and serve upon the defendant a motion for issuance of the Writ of Execution in accordance with Massachusetts General Laws c. 239 sec. 10.
7. The parties shall have all the rights and responsibilities specified in their lease except as modified by this agreement.
8. Other than as stipulated herein, the plaintiff waives all rights to evict the defendant for any and all incidents prior to the date of this agreement and hereby waives and releases unto the defendant any and all claims or actions arising out of the tenancy prior to the date of this agreement. The defendant hereby waives and releases unto the plaintiff any and all claims or actions arising out of the defendant's occupancy of the premises prior to the date of this agreement.

This agreement must be approved by a judge; and once approved, becomes a court order and both parties are legally required to follow it. I understand that I have a right to a hearing but instead choose to enter into this agreement.

Signed on this _____ day of April, 2015, under the pains and penalties of perjury

_____   _____
Plaintiff   Defendant

Stage 3: Trial day

In this stage, both the landlord and tenant appear in court. Because the parties in Stage 2 are negotiating an agreement enforceable by the court, they can reach this court enforceable agreement on any day up to trial day, or on the trial day itself, up to the moment the judge hears the case. In many court settings, when parties have reached their own agreements, the judge will ask the parties to appear in order to confirm that they have reached an agreement which they understand and which they agree shall be entered into the court record.

If the parties end up going before the judge, and particularly if substantive and procedural defenses are asserted, it is often in each party's interest to have legal counsel. Negotiation can still happen on trial day right up until the case is heard. The conversations presented in Stage 2 can happen during Stage 3. In Stage 3, however, the parties do prepare for trial, and in some cases, the parties will have the trial and receive the judge's decision.

---

*Questions for reflection: The Good Landlord
approach to eviction: Two-Track response*

---

1. Have you ever used any version of this Two-Track approach? What went
   well? What has been most difficult?

   _____
   _____
   _____
   _____
   _____
   _____

2. What challenges, if any, have you faced with issuing a notice to terminate
   tenancy? Could the ideas in this chapter help you overcome these
   challenges?

   _____
   _____
   _____
   _____
   _____
   _____

3. Do the sample conversations in this chapter make sense to you? Consider
   a tenant with whom you had or are having challenges. Would the
   conversations in this chapter help you get better results? Try writing
   down or speaking out loud the conversations you might have with your
   tenant.

   _____
   _____
   _____
   _____
   _____
   _____

12

Putting it all together

Is all this win-win stuff—enlightened self-interest, negotiation and all the rest—just talk? Don't you flat-out give up power when you share it with tenants? And isn't this the beginning of a well-known slippery slope? By now, we can expect these skeptical voices to have been reassured, at least a bit, as you have learned some psychologically-sound strategies, derived from real life scenarios, in which landlords on the brink have not only successfully avoided financial and personal disaster, but have improved their lot through a win-win method.

This book has approached the subject of helping landlords in a different way than other books. While the conventional wisdom is "don't be friends with your tenants," the preceding chapters have sketched out a more complex and, I believe, more accurate view. Friendship might not be the goal, but you are in relationship with your tenants, and the most effective strategies for property management turn out to be the ones that build the strongest relationships.

The methods outlined in these chapters do not always assume common interests. They certainly do not require friendship. What they demand is a steady, clear-minded presence, and an approach to landlording that resists the impulse to fight or to accommodate. They call for a recognition of two sets of interests, material and relational, which are interdependent but which must be untangled to be effectively addressed.

Your material *bottom line* interest is your own financial success, whether short- or long-term. Your enlightened self-interests, on the other hand, are represented by the quality of your relationships, particularly your ability to negotiate with your tenants, contractors, neighbors, family, friends, and everyone else, for that matter. If any of these interests are ignored, landlording can become quite unpleasant indeed.

These two kinds of interests (two kinds of wealth, we might say) have a lot to do with each other. The better you are doing financially, the more generous you can afford to be. The better you can communicate with tenants and maintain good tenancies, the lower your legal and management costs, and the more resources you will have to build your business. If more than a generation's worth of handling bitter housing battles has taught us anything, it is the business value of effective relationships. These are just a few of the selling points for the win-win model of problem solving.

Of course it is easiest to think in win-lose terms when you consider only time and money. If your costs remain fixed, you do not make any improvements, and you raise the rent, you are gaining while your tenant is losing. If, on the other hand, your revenues are fixed and a tenant with grievances files suit, this also has a win-lose feel to it. Committing to a win-win model, however, does not just mean adding more of one ingredient to the mix; you have to add additional ingredients which may not have been considered. Win-win thinking begins when you understand that ingredients other than income and expenses, such as the following, can make your business successful:

- Improved communication and ability to negotiate
- Enhanced credibility and respect
- Predictability and stability
- Minimized demands on your time and emotional energy
- Community goodwill
- Long-term business viability
- Satisfaction when you look yourself in the mirror

Seen this way, many elements of your success are shared with tenants. If you are a fairly conscientious landlord who raises rents only modestly, maintains your units and communicates well, staying in business preserves an important asset for tenants. Predictability and stability are as important to tenants as they are to landlords. So are simplicity and decreased demands on time and emotional energy. Virtually all of us, landlords and tenants alike, are stressed enough in our lives that minimizing conflict is a widely shared goal.

The landlord-tenant relationship is defined very tightly by the legal system and the rental-housing market. The challenges of maneuvering within these constraints are considerable. But, like it or not, your landlording approach makes a big impact on your tenants' lives. It is still within your power to interact in mutually beneficial ways.

If you happened to begin appreciating the principles laid out in this book before your tenants did, you may have an interest in doing some respectful but persistent tenant education. How can tenants—or anyone else, for that matter—learn to see their interests and yours as not being antagonistic? How can your tenants be helped to pursue negotiation when they are at risk of eviction, and they have legal leverage? If you are grappling with these questions, you are not alone. Landlords who have helped tenants move beyond fighting mode when eviction becomes a heated contest are still in the vanguard. But they have been at it long enough to point the way, and some aspects of the path are refreshingly simple. Like these landlords, you can:

- ❑ *Educate your tenants by sharing the principles you subscribe to and your reasons for thinking they work.* One of the wisest investments a good landlord can make is to hand out materials on conflict resolution and communication along with every lease, inviting tenants to consider learning and using these skills.
- ❑ *Start from the inside out:* Work first on your own resistance to communication, and your own anger and mistrust. This will certainly make you more skilled and credible in all your efforts. "Walking the talk," you become a role model for the type of behaviors you want to encourage. You also become more believable.
- ❑ *Help your tenants with some of their personal problems:* It is vital to do this without making your tenant dependent on you. You might want to steer tenants toward receiving income supports and various benefits, as well as counseling and human services, as part of an eviction prevention agreement. The difference between constructive help and "toxic help" can be as simple as the difference between driving the tenant to a job interview and driving her to the liquor store. One of the most important principles for landlords who choose to do some amount of "social work" is accountability: making sure your help is used responsibly. Of course, it is important to define accountability collaboratively, respecting your tenant's culture and values as well as your own.

The Good Landlord

❏ ***Formalize accountability and expectations in order to remove uncertainty:*** For example, there is no reason not to adapt your standard lease to include a commitment to negotiation and mediation before taking court action, and to carefully explain your reasons for doing so to tenants before they sign.

Bringing win-win principles into your dealings with tenants is part of a larger picture—the expanded notions of social responsibility and making a difference—which are gaining attention among property owners who recognize that their businesses are, after all, about providing a basic human need. This book has laid out a wide range of ways, built right into the landlord-tenant relationship, to make a difference. Additional examples of making a difference in the rental property business include:

❏ Contributing to community services such as leadership in crime watches and street or park cleaning
❏ Volunteering for causes one cares about
❏ Contributing a percentage of profits to community projects
❏ Profit-sharing with tenants in good standing, especially long-timers
❏ Contributing to any of a wide range of nonprofit organizations around the world

One long-time, large Cambridge, Massachusetts landlord I know has an even more radical vision: bringing landlords and tenants together into consumer cooperatives to buy commodities they all need, such as fuel oil and food, at lower cost.

All these ideas flow naturally from a handful of simple principles:

❏ Business success for a landlord is easiest when relationships with tenants are healthiest.
❏ Even though their interests diverge in some areas, landlords and tenants have many common interests.
❏ The range of common interests shared can be widened based on the quality of relationships between tenants and landlords.
❏ Using effective negotiation skills can often yield significant results over more adversarial means.

This does not mean that it is never necessary to set limits or take legal action. Eviction remains a powerful and sometimes necessary tool as discussed in Chapter 11. When dispute resolution is practiced effectively, however, eviction is used as a last resort, saving landlords money, time, and stress.

The potential for using the tools and skills introduced in this book is not just to make a profit, although profit is central. The tools and skills introduced can allow landlords, overall, to build community. And building community can serve as an antidote to unproductive conflict that puts both landlords and tenants, and the neighborhoods where they live, at risk. Perhaps this is why dispute resolution skills have become sought after in the 21st century. And, in contrast to many fields, you do not have to leave the work you are doing to practice it. Rarely has there been an approach that is so adaptable, and so appropriate just about anywhere.

Becoming a good landlord will help you not only to make a profit. Becoming a good landlord will make a difference in a world that will value the skills and experiences you have gained from providing for one of our most important needs: housing and home. For this, landlords do make a difference.

Appendices

Appendix A
A typology of landlords

A helpful framework for considering landlords' overall business motives comes from Jeanne Charn, Senior Lecturer on Law and Director, Bellow-Sacks Access to Civil Legal Services Project at Harvard Law School. She proposes four major types of landlords:

A typology of landlords

Developer/converter

▲ Can be large or small

▲ Buys low, converts, then sells high

▲ Puts little money into maintenance

Old-time slumlord

▲ Minimizes maintenance expenses

▲ "Milks" unit, then often abandons it

▲ Avoids legal requirements

Long-term residential, mixed income landlord

▲ Seeks long-term appreciation, not short-term gain

▲ Invests in maintenance and management

▲ Pursues long-term, stable tenancies using public funding whenever possible in order to preserve affordability

Owner-occupier or small landlord

▲ Owns one or a few properties only

▲ Buys a building to meet own housing expenses and to generate income

1. ***The developer/converter***, whose purpose is to buy at a low price and convert as quickly as possible to a luxury unit, condominium, or co-op for resale at a higher price, occupies a growing share of the housing market. He may be large or small. He tends to invest modest sums in maintenance of the units that remain in his control, holding on to some rental units as a source of working capital for upgrading others. Some are hands-on contractors and managers, while others are absent in their tenants' lives. The emphasis for these landlords is on renovation and conversion rather than maintaining current housing for tenants.

2. ***The old-time slumlord*** who "milks" units to their limit and then, frequently, abandons them to city control. This landlord owns substandard housing but, in contrast to the developer, does nothing to improve it, minimizing maintenance expenses and sidestepping legal requirements. These days, there are fewer landlords of this type, thanks to rental housing laws and tenant advocacy. Most city governments do catch up with their most flagrant slumlords.

3. ***The long-term residential mixed-income landlord*** who is motivated by the appreciation of an investment over years, rather than immediate gain. This landlord is law-abiding and responsible in maintenance of units. She rents to a mix of tenants, including those who receive federal or state rental assistance subsidies. Mixed-income landlords are typically torn between financial and social goals, all the more because their relationships with and concerns for their tenants are long-term. They may be drawn toward providing more luxury units to increase return on investment and to minimize the complexities that come with renting to low-income tenants. At the same time, many landlords in this group actively seek to preserve mixed-income housing.

4. ***The owner-occupier or small landlord*** who owns one or a few units and has bought property to meet his or her own housing needs. This landlord expects to pay the mortgage with rental income, and therefore lives with the interdependence of the landlord-tenant relationship in its most dramatic form. In Boston, small landlords control over half the rental housing stock, a significant enough share to exert some political and economic influence.

Appendix B

Preventing homelessness: How landlords help

Homeless!

Imagine yourself as a tenant (single mom and child) being evicted from her home one morning. You can also imagine yourself as a landlord, your house having just been foreclosed. Whether the bank, the landlord, a lawyer, a friend, or family member took the action, what is now happening to you is quite scary, overwhelming and unbearable. You are being forced out of your home!

Although the right to evict is a critical ingredient for success as a landlord, you can still appreciate what it could mean for tenants. Imagine, if you can, having exhausted all your housing options with literally no place to go. You have no family or friends to turn to, no new apartment, no money for anything, not even a motel room. The day turns dark and you have no idea where you and your child will sleep that night. The temperature is below freezing so sleeping outdoors is not an option. Finally, you locate a shelter and make your way there. You have no change of clothes, no money, not even a toothbrush. You are hungry, tired, angry, and depressed.

Sounds pretty horrible, doesn't it? Unfortunately, this nightmare is the reality of many, without the sigh of relief that comes with waking from a bad dream. It is no accident that many people cite the risk of homelessness as their greatest dread. And even for those who can crash for a few days on the sofa of a friend or family member, they face the prospect of having no place to live, prepare meals, get their mail, or leave their possessions. Every element of daily life that we who have homes take for granted is no longer there. And family members, including young children and spouses, are also affected. Imagine your kids being pulled from their school, without a home to go to.

Researchers tell us that on any given night, there are between 600,000 and 700,000 homeless people in the United States. A growing percentage of these people are families. Over two million people in this country will experience homelessness over the course of a year, and this figure rises during recessions.

These statistics tell a story of immense human suffering. What we often do not consider, however, is the significant public expense, borne by you and me. Whatever your political persuasion, all can appreciate how even the most bare bones entitlement spending can run up a large tab for the government. This spending includes:

The Good Landlord

❐ Emergency housing, transportation, and other services provided by some states when families are evicted
❐ Benefits, subsidies, and income supports for eligible individuals and families
❐ Human and social services
❐ Housing search focused on trying to get people back into decent housing and helping them to stay there

If they are not already employed, homeless people usually have overwhelming problems getting back into the job market and need a great deal of assistance in this area. Education is often needed. The costs of getting homeless individuals and families back on their feet again are enormous for any society.

Homelessness and its effects on families and children

What are the experiences of homeless families?

The negative effects experienced by homeless families are quite overwhelming and difficult to overcome.

> *"Families experiencing homelessness are under considerable stress. They may stay in multiple settings throughout the time they are without a home. Many double-up in overcrowded apartments with relatives and friends. Others sleep in cars and campgrounds or send their children to stay with relatives to avoid shelter life [if their children are not placed in foster care, from which many cannot return until their parent obtains housing]. Once in shelter, families must quickly adjust to overcrowded, difficult, and uncomfortable circumstances [and face environmental factors that can endanger their health]. Despite the efforts of dedicated staff, many*

SOURCE: *EXPERIENCES OF HOMELESS FAMILIES*

The National Center on Family Homelessness. *The Characteristics and Needs of Families Experiencing Homelessness.* Needham, MA: The National Center on Family Homelessness, December 2011.

shelters are noisy and chaotic; overcrowded and lacking privacy. Homelessness also increases the likelihood that families will separate or dissolve, which may compound the stress the family feels."

Homelessness and children

"Homeless children are not simply at risk; most suffer specific physical, psychological, and emotional damage due to the circumstances that accompany episodes of homelessness....Homelessness influences every facet of a child's life—from conception to young adulthood. The experience of homelessness inhibits the physical, emotional, cognitive, social, and behavioral development of children."

Early years

"Children born into homelessness are more likely to have low birth weights and are at greater risk of [sickness and] death.... Homeless children begin to demonstrate significant developmental delays after 18 months of age, which are believed to influence later behavioral and emotional problems....Despite these developmental delays and emotional difficulties, homeless [children] receive fewer [health and education] services than other children their age. By the time homeless children reach school age, their homelessness affects their social, physical, and academic lives...."

Physical and emotional health and behavior

"In general, homeless children consistently exhibit more health problems than housed poor children... Homeless children are at greater risk for [infectious disease], asthma and lead poisoning,... poor nutrition...stunted growth and anemia... [They're also] confronted with stressful and traumatic events that they often are too young to understand, leading to severe emotional distress. Homeless children experience stress through constant changes, which accumulate with time. These stressful changes result in a higher incidence of mental disorders, which become manifested in homeless children's behavior."

SOURCE: ***HOMELESSNESS AND CHILDREN***

Ellen Hart-Shegos. *Homelessness and its Effects on Children*. Minneapolis, MN: Family Housing Fund, 1999.

Academic development

"Homeless children's academic performance is hampered both by their poor cognitive development and by the circumstances of their homelessness, such as constant mobility. Homeless children are more likely to score poorly on math, reading, spelling, and vocabulary tests and are more likely to be held back a year in school."

These are just a few examples of how homelessness can adversely affect the health and well-being of children and families.

Home and community

When landlords provide shelter, they are providing a fundamental human need. Shelter represents a basic element for individuals and families to survive in this world. A home is where many essential activities are conducted, such as food preparation, recreation, family life, rest and renewal—the list is quite long. A majority of Americans interviewed say that their home, however humble, is the single most secure and safe place they know. It is the place where we feel most grounded, most "at home." It is also the place where many of life's activities occur. Whether you are a landlord or tenant, home is your base.

Having a home, at its core, is about avoiding homelessness. But it is also about building a life and thriving in the wider world. Where you live— particularly if you are poor or a person of color—can limit how much of society's benefits you can reap. Living in a bad neighborhood without decent housing may limit your ability to secure quality education for your children, a decent job for yourself, and access to good public services. Decent housing, advocates argue, can promote dignity, self-respect and hope, with added opportunities for good education, health and employment—all the things people need to get ahead in our society. Where one lives makes a profound difference in the potential for human success or failure.

Home as a refuge

Amia Lieblich, an Israeli psychologist who helps traumatized people return to feeling normal in daily life, in a telephone interview said, "Home is a place with the reservoir of our good memories. It has all kinds of symbols of the past, like our pictures and books. It's where we have our relationships and routines. When there is a war going on, women cook and bake more. Home is not a perfect refuge, of course. It bedevils us with unfinished projects and aggravating repairs. [But] it can be a real haven."

Some examples of what good housing can provide

- ❐ ***The ability to avoid homelessness.*** The landlord's capacity to keep rent at reasonable levels, particularly for low-income tenants, can make the difference between their having or not having a home.
- ❐ ***Adequate, habitable housing conditions.*** For tenants who come from a low-income background, this may be the first decent living space they have ever had.
- ❐ ***Educational achievement.*** By staying in the same schools over time, made possible through adequate housing, tenants' children can thrive in school and ultimately get ahead in life.
- ❐ ***Access to good work.*** This comes from maintaining a stable home life in a stable neighborhood.
- ❐ ***An opportunity to build community.*** Stable housing provides families the possibility of staying where they are long enough to cultivate neighborhood ties, get involved in their community, and feel like they belong somewhere.
- ❐ ***Community revitalization.*** When landlords maintain their buildings and grounds, and participate in local improvement projects, tenants reap the benefits of having entire neighborhoods develop and thrive.
- ❐ ***Lower crime*** than in areas with boarded-up houses.

As you can see, the stakes are quite high. Tenants can reap the highest rewards of society when landlords provide decent housing. This is why it is so important for landlords to find a way to succeed as housing providers.

Maslow's hierarchy of needs

Abraham Maslow (1908–1970) is considered the founder of humanistic psychology. He is especially noted for his ideas concerning human motivation. It is interesting to note where housing, or shelter, is on Maslow's "hierarchy of needs."

Shelter ranks as one of the most fundamental needs, at the base of Maslow's hierarchy. However, as we have discussed in this chapter, housing can also contribute to all of the "higher order needs." These include personal safety, a sense of belonging (to a neighborhood), and self-esteem from living in decent housing. A stable home provided by a landlord provides the base from which tenants can meet their needs and pursue the goals they most want for themselves and for their families and wider communities.

Hierarchy of needs

Higher order needs

- ▲ **Self-actualization needs:** *creativity, purpose, meaning, morality, being the best person one can be in the service of self and others;*
- ▲ **Cognitive needs:** *knowledge, understanding, exploration*
- ▲ **Aesthetic needs:** *beauty, balance, order*
- ▲ **Esteem needs:** *respect and esteem from and for others and self, feelings of accomplishment, achievement, recognition*
- ▲ **Love and belonging needs:** *appreciation, acceptance, friendship, intimacy, love*
- ▲ **Safety needs:** *security in body, resources, morality, family, health, property; order, limits*
- ▲ **Physiological needs (for basic survival):** *food, water, air, sleep, clothing, warmth, shelter*

Lower order needs

The role of small landlords in providing affordable housing

What role do small landlords play as housing providers? When small landlords run their buildings well, they contribute enormously to providing decent, affordable housing and preventing homelessness. Stabilizing these small rental properties and their landlords should be a priority for cities across the United States as a way to strengthen neighborhoods, prevent urban deterioration, and prevent homelessness. Consider the following facts and figures about the contributions made by small landlords to America's housing sector.

Small rental properties form the backbone of the US housing stock

Contrary to popular views, most rental housing is not in high-density buildings. More than half of all rentals are in small structures, including single-family homes and 2–4 unit buildings. Another quarter of the housing stock is in multifamily buildings with 5–19 units, with the rest equally divided between large structures with 20–49 units and 50 or more units.

Distribution of rental housing stock by property type, 2000

Category	Number of Units	Percentage of Total
1 unit, detached	8,531,853	23.9%
1 unit, attached	2,087,994	5.9
2 units	3,301,854	9.3
3 to 4 units	4,254,351	11.9
5 to 9 units	4,332,461	12.1
10 to 19 units	3,748,728	10.5
20 to 49 units	3,049,458	8.6
50 or more units	4,798,031	13.5
Mobile home, RV or boat	1,558,858	4.4
TOTAL	**35,663,588**	**100%**

SOURCE: DISTRIBUTION OF RENTAL HOUSING

US Census, 2000, cited in Alan Mallach, *Landlords at the Margins: Exploring the Dynamics of the One To Four Unit Rental Housing Industry* (Cambridge, MA: Joint Center for Housing Studies, Harvard University, 2007), 2. www.jchs.harvard.edu. All rights reserved.

Individuals, not corporate entities, own a significant share of small rental properties

Individuals own about 85% of 2–4 unit rental properties in the United States and, by contrast, only about 9% of 50+ unit rental properties.

Share of rental units owned by individuals, 2001

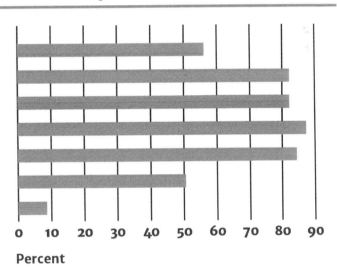

SOURCE: **SHARE OF RENTAL UNITS OWNED BY INDIVIDUALS**

Harvard Joint Center for Housing Studies tabulations of U.S. Census Bureau 2001 Residential Finance Survey. Joint Center for Housing Studies of Harvard University, *America's Rental Housing—Meeting Challenges, Building on Opportunities* (Cambridge, MA: Joint Center for Housing Studies of Harvard University, 2011), 22. www.jchs.harvard.edu. All rights reserved.

The Good Landlord

Many small landlords historically have been long-term owners, holding onto their properties for rental and retirement income, and for housing for themselves and their families

Although recent data indicates a trend towards more speculative behavior, Mallach, based on the *1995 Property Owners and Managers Survey* (POMS) data, notes, "The typical property owner has held her property for 10 years or more... and has no plans to sell within the next five years." (Mallach, 26) A substantial percentage of these small landlords are "inadvertent" landlords who "backed into" the business of property ownership. (Mallach, 27–28)

Most one- to four-family rental properties are managed by their owners

"84% of the owners of single family detached, as well as 2–4 family, properties manage their own properties," writes Mallach (34). How much time do they spend managing their properties? Mallach cites POMS data showing that "the great majority of owners spend little time managing their properties," but concludes, based on his own interviews, that most landlords who manage their one- to four-family rental properties "devoted a good deal of time to property management, although in an unsystematic fashion." (Mallach, 34–36) He explains this, stating: "Few owners actually collect a salary for their work, and it is likely that the majority make little or no attempt to account for their time spent on property management and maintenance." (Mallach, 38)

Rents are more affordable for unsubsidized tenants because many of their small landlords are less profit-oriented

Many small landlords are part-timers, needing to work elsewhere for their primary income. The POMS findings confirm this: "Fewer than 40% of the owners of one to four family rental properties reported that they had made a profit on their property during the preceding year." (Mallach, 31)

Given this scenario, how do small landlords sustain themselves as property owners? Many spend much less per unit overall than do larger owners, treating their time as a form of sweat equity rather than as a billable cost or overhead. These small landlords minimize spending in order to keep rents low and avoid vacancies. As Mallach states: "In the final analysis, a low ratio of maintenance and management expenses to rental income is a threshold condition of the viability of the one to four family rental industry." (Mallach, 38) Because many of their small landlords are less profit-oriented, rents, thus, are typically more affordable for unsubsidized tenants.

SOURCES

1995 Property Owners and Managers Survey www.census.gov/housing/poms/

Alan Mallach, *Landlords at the Margins: Exploring the Dynamics of the One to Four Unit Rental Housing Industry* (Cambridge, MA: Joint Center for Housing Studies, Harvard University, 2007), www.jchs.harvard.edu.

The Good Landlord

What do we mean by "affordable housing"?

There is a great deal of discussion in American society these days about what is meant by "affordable" as it relates to housing and homelessness prevention. Whereas for some tenants, a comfortable house with a good-sized backyard in an upper-middle class suburb is affordable; for others, even a small place needing some maintenance in a run-down neighborhood may not be affordable. There are substantial differences in what people can pay for housing.

In housing parlance, however, the word "affordable" has often been equated with the use of a public subsidy. City, state or federal affordable housing plans generally link the use of a public subsidy to the definition of affordable. In some cases the subsidy is built right into the building's operating income stream, making units affordable for whoever qualifies to live in them. In other cases, the tenant brings the subsidy to the unit—for example, in the form of a mobile Section 8 housing voucher. Whether attached to the building or to the tenant, these subsidies involve the use of public dollars.

Many landlords, however, can and do provide housing that is affordable without the use of a subsidy. Some landlords, particularly smaller ones, consider the incomes of their tenants and adjust their rents to help their tenants be able to afford to pay. These landlords will also work with tenants to allow them to pay any back rent owed over time. They may accommodate other reasonable ideas such as bartering for rent or allowing additional occupants in order to make affordable housing possible. This additional definition of "affordable housing," to include housing provided without a subsidy, contributes in a major way to America's affordable housing stock.

For the majority of tenants, whether or not they have a subsidy, a successful relationship with their landlord can be a big factor in preventing homelessness. The landlord's choice to keep rent levels within reason and to "work with" tenants when they fall behind also makes this possible. Helping landlords to make a profit, while providing affordable housing for low- and moderate-income tenants, has been a focus of this book. One of the ways this can be accomplished is to help landlords learn the basics of property management. At the same time, learning the skills of managing relationships and resolving conflict can make providing affordable housing easier, less expensive, and more profitable for landlords.

A Guide to Making a Profit While Making a Difference

Questions for reflection: Preventing homelessness: How landlords help

---

1. Think of your own experiences of home and its meaning in your daily life. What does home mean to you?

   _____

   _____

   _____

2. What if you didn't have a home? Have you ever thought about what it would be like to be homeless?

   _____

   _____

   _____

3. Do you see people who are homeless in your daily life? Do you know anyone who has ever been homeless? What are your thoughts about this?

   _____

   _____

   _____

4. Look again at Maslow's hierarchy of needs. List as clearly as possible the needs that you would like to have met for you as a landlord. What plans could enhance your meeting these needs? Now think about your tenants. What needs might they want met in their role as tenants? How might you be able to help them meet these needs in a way that honors your own needs?

   _____

   _____

   _____

5. What is different about providing housing as a small property owner rather than as a large property owner? Are there any unique contributions that you provide as a landlord?

   _____

   _____

   _____

Appendix C
Mindfulness: An introduction

Wherever you go, there you are.

> *John Kabat–Zinn*
> *Professor of Medicine Emeritus and creator of*
> *the Stress Reduction Clinic*
> *and the Center for Mindfulness in Medicine,*
> *Health Care, and Society*
> *at the University of Massachusetts*
> *Medical School*
> *Worcester, Massachusetts*

Mindfulness can be of tremendous use for managing stressful situations effectively by helping you to understand and harness your thoughts and emotions. This appendix will introduce mindfulness, a practice for simply being aware in the present moment and using one's awareness skillfully. Mindfulness is a profoundly useful tool for all aspects of life, including landlording. It can be especially useful when diffusing landlord-tenant situations that are potentially explosive.

Practice mindfulness

A number of communication approaches are presented in this book. A personal practice underlying each of them, which can make a significant difference for landlords, is called mindfulness.

Mindfulness is the kind of practice that can dramatically improve your communication with your tenants, and your handling of people issues in general. I know this from my own experience, and hope that you may discover this for yourself as well. Let's explore mindfulness by first understanding what happens without it.

Mindlessness

Have you ever grabbed a bite to eat from the fridge and, while you were chewing, become aware that you had not decided you really wanted to eat this food? Or maybe you have been leafing through a magazine only to realize that you had not really decided to read. I think you will agree that

---

DEFINITION: **MINDFULNESS**

Mindfulness refers to being completely in touch with and aware of the present moment, as well as taking a non-evaluative and non-judgmental approach to your inner experience. For example, a mindful approach to one's inner experience is simply viewing "thoughts as thoughts" as opposed to evaluating them as positive or negative.

all of us have experienced these lapses in attention. These are common examples of mindlessness or going on automatic pilot.

We all experience moments of inattention, which result in our not being fully present for what we are thinking, feeling, and doing in our own lives. The consequences of being inattentive can sometimes be quite costly, resulting in our missing some really good experiences and ignoring important information and messages about our own lives and our relationships.

Our reactions to stressful events as landlords can become so habitual that they occur outside of our awareness, until the neglected situations become serious enough that we can't ignore them any longer. These mindless reactions can cause body tension and painful emotions, including depression, rage and at times, even panic. We can become prisoners of our own obsessive thinking and self-criticism. These habits can also motivate us, furthermore, to seek revenge. By being more mindful, however, we can avoid stewing in our own anger and instead learn more effective ways to solve problems.

Mindfulness: Awareness in the present moment

A remedy for this tendency to be inattentive and allow anger to overwhelm us is to practice mindfulness. Mindfulness is a practice of paying careful attention, something we almost always have the ability to learn to do even more carefully. Mindfulness is the quality of basic awareness of, or attention to, what is happening to us right now, inside our bodies and in our immediate environment. Whether we pay more attention to sights, sounds, smells, tastes, sensations, or thoughts, mindfulness allows us to discern, from a quieter place within, what words to say or actions to take.

For those who may be practicing mindfulness, whether they know it or not, there are many moments during the day when it can come in handy. When my son raised his voice at me the other day, for example, and I felt the heat rising from within, I tried to be mindful. I let myself feel the sensations—in my body and mind as I concocted my angry response—without raising my fists, let alone interrupting his anger in order to inject mine. I was able to let him finish his thought, ask him some questions, reflect back what I heard, and then carefully respond in a way that really mattered—and that he heard. I had few regrets about how I acted or what I said.

As a landlord, you can practice mindfulness as one way to become more aware of what is happening in your business. You can try to ground your attention in the present moment and allow yourself to be more aware of what is happening now. You can become more interested in just knowing what is happening than in reacting to it. In this way, you don't just get caught up in emotional responses. You can pay attention without trying to change anything. You can be calmer and more effective in any situation, including in your role as a landlord.

To the extent that you pay more attention to "being," your "doing" will be better informed, more responsive, and less driven by the habits of reaction and inattention.

How can you practice mindfulness? Your first step is to make the effort! Whenever you think of it, day or night, remember that you can be more mindful. See for yourself what it is like to be in the present and pay more careful attention to what is here, especially what you are experiencing in your own body, heart, and mind. You can practice mindfulness at any time: at the start of a new activity or at the end of it, when you are doing something intensely or resting after work. Introduced below are a few hints for becoming acquainted with this profoundly important practice.

To get started, find a place to be stationary, whether sitting, standing, or lying down. Then, use the sensation of your breath as the "anchor" for awareness in the present moment. You can establish mindfulness simply by focusing on the sensation of breathing. Pay attention to the actual sensation of your breath as it goes in and goes out, and the pause between your in-breath and your out-breath. Don't try to control your breath, but simply let it come and go. Bring as much attention to the direct sensation of your breath as completely and continuously as you can.

After a while, if you wish, when you have established awareness of the sensation of breathing, you might widen the focus to include all body sensations. Again, avoid trying to change anything at all! Instead, simply allow yourself to feel and to be aware of the changing sensations in your body.

Anytime you feel lost, confused, or frustrated, gently remember to be aware of the sensation of your breath. You may have to do this frequently. The important thing is the quality of awareness you bring to the moment. One moment of mindfulness, one breath when you are truly present, can make a big difference. See for yourself!

You can practice mindfulness in this way at any time. Try just a few breaths at a time, just a few mindful moments. If you wish, you can make this a more formal practice by regularly setting aside some time (from a few minutes to a half hour or more) free from other activity or distractions during which you can devote your full attention to simply being mindful of what is present. Over time, you will find that a formal practice of mindfulness can support and strengthen your ability to handle challenging situations, with tenants, with parts of yourself, or anyone else!

Hints

Expect your mind to wander! Especially if you practice for only a few breaths or for a few minutes, be kind and patient with yourself when you become distracted, and gently return awareness to the breath sensation. Be aware of any tendency to be hard on yourself or to feel frustrated at your failure to be present. View this kind of judgment as just another kind of thinking, and gently return awareness to the breath.

Expect to feel some relaxation, especially if you practice for even a few breaths or for a few moments. This relaxed feeling is an ally. It can help you be more present, more mindful. Relaxation alone, however, is not what mindfulness is about. It is about being present with awareness.

Expect to become more mindful with practice. Expect to notice more things, including difficult things. This is actually progress! You are not doing anything wrong. Quite the opposite—you are increasing your mindfulness for all things. Be careful, though, to avoid practicing too hard. Don't try to make anything happen, or to achieve any particular result. Simply relax and pay as much attention as you can to what is happening here and now.

Applying mindfulness as a landlord

There are many times when mindfulness can make an enormous difference to you as a landlord. Mindfulness can help you learn to consider more carefully what to say before speaking, particularly when you are angry. This

The Good Landlord

is immensely useful and can help you avoid saying or doing things you will regret later.

Mindfulness can also be an effective tool to help you to clarify what you want, prepare to engage, and then communicate effectively. Adopting a mindful approach may be a constant challenge, but it is one that will bring great benefits to you as a landlord. This approach may also affect other aspects of your life, making all of your relationships more pleasant and constructive.

READING RESOURCES

Joseph Goldstein and Jack Kornfield, *Seeking the Heart of Wisdom: The Path of Insight Meditation* (Boston, MA: Shambhala, 1987).

Bhante Henepola Gunaratana, *Mindfulness in Plain English* (Somerville, MA: Wisdom Publications, 2002).

Jack Kornfield, *The Wise Heart: A Guide to the Universal Teachings of Buddhist Psychology* (New York: Random House, 2008).

Jack Kornfield, *A Path with Heart: A Guide Through the Perils and Promises of Spiritual Life* (New York: Bantam Books, 1993).

Sharon Salzberg, *A Heart As Wide As the World: Stories on the Path of Lovingkindness* (Boston: Shambhala, 1999).

Appendix D
Dispute Resolution Prep Sheet

Instructions

Use this worksheet (and more paper as necessary) to help you think through your plans for resolving difficult issues with your tenant. You may find it useful to do this exercise again as the situation evolves. Re-evaluating new situations can often be quite helpful.

The Good Landlord

1. *What is your legal situation? What legal risks do you face? What legal risks does your tenant face? What do you understand would be most likely to happen if a judge decided the case?*

   _____

   _____

   _____

   _____

2. *What are your interests? Reduce the number of occupants? Get compensation for property damage? Eviction? Payment plan for the back rent? Rent increase? Clarify your interests and list them from most to least important.*

   _____

   _____

   _____

3. *Determine which is more important to you—time or money? If you want a tenant to move out, for example, you may need to offer more money. How much back rent would you be agreeable to give up to get a faster move-out date?*

   _____

   _____

   _____

4. *What are your tenant's interests? To avoid paying some rent? To have a more predictable access plan? To increase the number of occupants to reduce individual costs? Clarify what you understand to be his or her interests.*

   _____

   _____

   _____

5. *What is this dispute really about? Is it "just" about nonpayment or whether or not the unit is worth a higher rent? Or, is it about retribution by the tenant because of past landlord-tenant issues? How much of the dispute is about interests and how much is about hard feelings?*

   _____

   _____

   _____

6. Is your tenant at risk of homelessness? Have there been any concerns directed at you as a landlord other than from the tenant? Will your actions be interpreted negatively or positively by those who may be aware of your dispute?

_____

_____

_____

7. What aspects of the public interest enter into this dispute? Have you considered what the public impact could be, positively or negatively, from your landlording approach?

_____

_____

_____

8. What involvement of helpers (lawyers, advocates, friends) do you need? How much should you use them? What help should you get? What specific tasks should they do for you?

_____

_____

_____

9. How much has the dispute escalated? What skills and capabilities do you and the tenant have to resolve the dispute yourselves? What incentives are in place to resolve the conflict before court?

_____

_____

_____

Appendix E
Eviction procedures in Massachusetts and other states

In Massachusetts, landlord-tenant relationships and eviction procedures are mostly governed by M.G.L. Chapters 186 (Estates for Years and At Will) and 239 (Summary Process for Possession of Land), as well as Massachusetts Rules of Court, Uniform Summary Process Rules.

Usually, a landlord starts an eviction by serving on the tenant a Notice to Quit. If the reason is for nonpayment, the tenant is given 14 days' notice. For most other reasons, the tenant must be given 30 days' notice. In nonpayment cases, the tenant has 10 days from receiving the notice to "cure" his lack of payment and thus stop the eviction. The law is very specific that the notice must inform the tenant of this right. If the tenant does not pay, after 14 days have elapsed the landlord then may serve the tenant with a Summary Process Summons and Complaint, which sets out the trial date and date by which the tenant must file an Answer if he so chooses. In the case of a 30-day notice, the Summons is the same; the only difference is that the landlord must wait for the 30 days to elapse.

If there is a judgment for the landlord, there is a 10-day appeal period. If the tenant does not appeal during that time, the court will then issue a Writ of Execution, which enables the landlord to hire a deputy sheriff or constable to enforce the writ, by presenting it to the tenant or posting it. After 48 hours, the sheriff or constable may physically remove the tenant (if she's still there) and any possessions left behind. The landlord is required to have possessions stored in a bonded warehouse for 90 days (which the landlord must pay for up front). If after 90 days the tenant does not pay to remove them from storage, the landlord or warehouse is free to dispose of the possessions.

Most other states have similar concepts in their eviction procedures—a written notice followed by a Summons to court, and after a judgment, physical removal by some sort of officer—marshal, court officer, or sheriff, depending on the state. The main differences among the states are the lengths of the notice periods. For example, in **New Hampshire**, a landlord gives seven days' notice if the reason is nonpayment, the tenant's behavior is harming the health or safety of the landlord or other tenants, or the tenant has substantially damaged the premises; in all other cases,

The Good Landlord

a landlord must give 30 days' notice (although, unlike in **Massachusetts**, the landlord must always state a reason for the eviction). As with nonpayment cases in **Massachusetts**, the tenant has a right to cure the situation and notice of this right must be in the notice to vacate. Also as in **Massachusetts**, once the notice period has expired, a sheriff serves the tenant with a Summons, but if the tenant does not file an appearance by the return date (when an Answer is due), there is no hearing and the tenant is notified by mail that he has lost. If he does file his appearance, there is a hearing; if he requests Discovery, he must do so within five days after the return date, and the landlord has 14 days to comply; if the landlord does not comply, the tenant can get the trial postponed. If the landlord wins the case, the court issues a Writ of Possession three days after the judgment. If the tenant has left possessions behind, the landlord must take care of them for 28 days, after which he can dispose of them without notice to the tenant. Another difference in **New Hampshire** is that if the landlord suffers monetary damages (such as unpaid rent or property damage), she cannot ask for more than $1,500 in damages. If her actual damages exceed that, she may sue separately, in small claims court. The **New Hampshire** statute emphasizes the landlord-tenant relationship over financial loss.

For comparison: in **New York**, nonpayment evictions are given three days' notice, with 10 days' notice for most other situations; if the landlord wins, a warrant of possession is issued, which gives the tenant 72 hours to leave or be removed by a marshal. In **New Jersey**, notice is three days for nonpayment or "substantial" lease violations, otherwise one rental period; if the landlord wins, the court issues a warrant of possession, which a court officer can act on 3 business days after the judgment. In **New Mexico**, it is three days' notice for nonpayment or "knowingly" committing a "substantial violation of the law," seven days for lease violations or "other unlawful conduct," and 30 days for most other situations; if the landlord prevails, the court sets an eviction date three to seven days after the judgment, which is enforced by a sheriff acting on a writ of restitution. In **Arkansas**, the notice period is one rental period for most cases, three days for nonpayment, and in certain situations a tenant may even be charged with a misdemeanor (lesser crime) for unlawful failure to vacate; and all tenant property left behind is deemed abandoned, which the landlord may lien for unpaid rent. In **Alabama**, notice for nonpayment is seven days, for lease violation 14 days, and in most other cases 30 days; also, a landlord may be entitled to double the rent for holdover tenants and a lien on property left behind for unpaid rent. If the tenant is a "willful" holdover, the landlord may even get up to three months' rent as damages, plus attorney's fees. In **California**, notice is three days for nonpayment, and some local laws provide that if a tenant has lived in the premises for more than one year, 60 days' notice is required (if nonpayment is NOT the issue). If the tenancy is greater than two years, the landlord must state a "good cause" to evict.

In summary, wherever you own property, it is vital to be as familiar as possible with all applicable laws (local, county, state, and federal), since they all have their quirks and even a technical violation can be very costly to a landlord.

Appendix F
Analytical table of contents

The Good Landlord

The Good Landlord

The Good Landlord

Index

The Good Landlord

For over 25 years, Peter Gilman Shapiro has been empowering landlords to make a profit while making a difference in their communities.

A graduate of MIT's Master's Program in City Planning, Peter went on to found and direct the Housing Services Program at Just-A-Start Corporation, a nonprofit in Cambridge, Massachusetts. From 1990 to 2015, Peter and his team provided mediation, legal services, and training, and led support groups for landlords across Massachusetts. His innovative techniques led to the successful resolution of thousands of disputes regarding eviction, housing, real estate, business, and family matters.

A landlord himself, Peter has been developing, testing, and applying the ideas set forth in this book with his own tenants since 1990.

Peter continues to provide mediation, training, and consulting, nationwide, on how to:

- build productive landlord-tenant relationships
- communicate and negotiate effectively
- prevent tenant issues from escalating into costly disputes
- address eviction in a sensible way

Peter lives in the Jamaica Plain neighborhood of Boston, Massachusetts with his two teenage sons and his partner, Aline.

Visit his website, www.thegoodlandlord.com, or contact him at peter@thegoodlandlord.com.

Made in the USA
Middletown, DE
05 January 2018